Homemade Hospitality

Opening Your Heart and Your Home to Others

BARBARA SIMS

PROMISE
PRESS
An Imprint of Barbour Publishing

ISBN 1-58660-146-6

Published by Promise Press, an imprint of Barbour Publishing, Inc., PO Box 719, Uhrichsville, Ohio 44683, www.promisepress.com

Member of the
Evangelical Christian
Publishers Association

Printed in the United States of America.

Dedication

For Don,
my husband and encourager
who freely opens his heart to me
and to all those who enter the doors of our home.

Contents

Acknowledgments

Recognizing that many contributed to make *Homemade Hospitality* a reality, it is with gratitude that I acknowledge friends and family members for opening the gates of their hospitality gardens and sharing their stories: the G.I.R.L.S. (Gab, Indulge, Relax, Laugh, and Share) Group for bravely confessing their hospitality bloopers; Don for being patient and supportive each time he found me drowning in manuscript revisions; Margery for editing, supporting, and encouraging; and Susan, my editor, for trusting me with this special project.

To each reader. . .

"I pray that Christ will be
more and more at home in your hearts."
EPHESIANS 3:17 TLB

What in the World Has Happened?

Share with God's people. . . .
Practice hospitality.
ROMANS 12:13 NIV

Mama baked cookies and the back door was always open at our house. A light tap by a neighbor's hand on the screened porch door was quickly followed by my mother's voice singing, "Come on in." During cold months, chocolate was simmering on the stove; summer temperatures demanded iced tea for adults, and Mama served thirsty children Kool-Aid in multicolored aluminum tumblers that dripped with condensation. Toll House Chocolate Chip Cookies were seasonless.

PRACTICAL POINTERS

Revive an old tradition and use this recipe to keep chocolate chip cookies on hand for any children—or adults—who wander past your home:

²/₃ cup shortening
²/₃ cup softened butter
  or margarine
1 cup sugar
1 cup packed brown sugar
2 eggs
2 tsp vanilla

3 cups flour
1 tsp soda
1 tsp salt
1 cup chopped nuts
  (optional)
1 package (12 oz)
  semisweet
  chocolate chips

Mix shortening, butter, eggs, sugars, and vanilla. Add other ingredients. (If you add an additional ½ cup flour, it will make a softer, thicker cookie.) Drop dough by rounded teaspoons onto ungreased baking sheet. Bake 8–10 minutes at 375 degrees or until light brown. Makes about 7 dozen cookies.

Our screened front porch was the popular spot on hot and sultry Southern evenings. Grown-ups chatted about the happenings of the day and discussed the weather, which usually was too hot, too humid, or too dry. Noisy children chased lightning bugs or played hide-and-seek in the dark front yard.

Grandparents and other close relatives lived with us from time to time, and our home was a natural place for many others to gather. My mother was the oldest daughter in a family of twelve children, and her younger siblings came to visit often, bringing their children to play. When my father's family from the country came, they brought cooked food and lots of cousins. Hospitality was never discussed; as a child, I doubt I ever heard the word. It was just a way of life.

Soon after our soldiers returned from fighting a war on foreign soil, without warning (and with little notice) dramatic changes took place on the home front. Lifestyles changed almost overnight. Cars and planes took us anywhere we wanted to go. When we chose to stay at home, we simply pushed a button and television brought an ever-expanding world into our living room. We sat down in an easy chair, picked up a remote control and a dish of ice cream, and overindulged. We closed and locked our doors securely, and the rhythmic squeak of a porch swing was replaced by the intermittent hum of an air-conditioning unit.

Next-door neighbors became nameless strangers who didn't make eye contact with anyone during their once-a-day outside excursion to pick up the morning paper. Surrounded by dozens of laborsaving devices, we no longer had time to bake cookies. The absence of cookies did not matter so much, though, because no one knocked on the locked back door.

A constantly enlarging transient society depended on Ma Bell to "reach out and touch." More recently the U.S. Mail has been replaced with E-mail. Having lost the sound of our friends' voices and the joy of opening handwritten letters, we now connect with others electronically. We E-mail messages to people five thousand miles away, and yet we do not speak to our neighbor next door.

As we plunge into a new century, many adults cannot accurately define hospitality without the aid of a dictionary. Both parents and children live in the fast lane.

And if my mother were alive today, she would likely ask, "What in this world has happened?"

Of course, few would want to return to cooking

on a wood-burning stove, sending telegrams, or traveling by horse and carriage. The advantages of our technological world are wonderful. (Those of us in the South especially appreciate air-conditioning.) But as we enter another century, many, both the young and the old, are giving our busy way of life a second thought. We long to slow down, sit down, and just visit for a while. We want to recapture a time when life was simpler, when people had time for each other, when hospitality—"the welcoming and entertaining of guests that comes from a heart of love"—was practiced. Back then we didn't need to define the word.

If you would like an opportunity to return to the warmth of yesteryear, if you want to be reminded of what the Bible has to say about hospitality, this book was written just for you. As you turn these pages, my prayer is that your heart will be touched and you will open the doors of your home to others.

GLIMPSES
The ornaments of a house are the friends who frequent it.

RALPH WALDO EMERSON

The Bear Story
(or Take the First Step)

Offer hospitality to one another. . . .
1 PETER 4:9 NIV

Hospitality is sort of like the weather. Everybody talks about it. Newsstands display magazines with bright covers and pages filled with ideas for entertaining. Daily newspapers print recipes describing tantalizing food to serve to all our guests. The nation focuses on entertaining. Almost everyone *plans* to have a party or invite a couple for dinner. We just never *do* it!

I am reminded of the bear story. A mama bear had a baby cub, and it was time for the cub to learn to walk. The baby cub asked his mama, "Do I put both of my front feet on the ground to start walking? Or should I start with my back feet? Maybe it would be better to use one front foot and one back foot?" The mother bear listened patiently, then replied, "Just stop talking and start walking."

Likewise I challenge you to "stop talking and start inviting!" If you wait until the house is remodeled, the flower garden is at its peak, and all the children are well behaved, your doorbell will never ring.

In our "I, Me, and Mine" society, it is easier and more comfortable to live selfishly, to leave the doors closed and the curtains drawn. But hospitality is the extreme opposite of selfishness. Changes in hearts should bring changes in behavior. Yet many who have experienced the forgiveness of Christ continue to live and behave selfishly. If we follow Christ's example, we will open doors and welcome others to enter.

Stop talking and start inviting.

PRACTICAL POINTERS

Perhaps you have a friend who has lost a loved one. Maybe you have prayed for her or even mailed a card. Pick up the phone, dial her number, and ask when she can come for a visit. No need to clean house, cook a meal, or even bake a cookie. Just open the door to your home. Serve tea. Hot or cold, tea always seems to warm relationships. Listen if she needs to talk. Tell her you care. Give her a hug before she leaves. Let her know your door is open and invite her to return.

Call a couple, or a friend, and invite them to dinner. Buy some colorful paper napkins. Cook a simple meal, perhaps your favorite casserole, a vegetable, and a salad. Pick up some rolls from the grocery and a frozen fruit pie for dessert. Be sure you've got vanilla ice cream in the freezer. It's amazing how quickly you become motivated to cook when you know hungry guests will arrive at an appointed hour! Greet your guests with a smile—and then relax and enjoy yourself. If you have a good time, your guests will also enjoy themselves.

Or you might invite your neighbors, the ones who moved on your block about two years ago whom you still have not met. Serve lemonade and brownies on the porch if the weather is warm or cider and oatmeal cookies by the fire after the first frost.

If you are over forty, invite a young married couple to your home for a sit-down dinner. Treat them special with place cards, china and silver, and service with a smile. They will love being pampered. If you are under forty, invite an older couple with no family nearby to celebrate a holiday in your home. Or invite them for dinner and an old movie.

Do something! Stop talking and start inviting!

Hospitality is not an isolated event. Rather it is a lifestyle. And if you choose to do so, you can make it your lifestyle. Become a trendsetter for the twenty-first century. Rediscover hospitality.

GLIMPSES

*Love doesn't just sit there like a stone,
it has to be made, like bread.*

URSULA K. LEGUIN

Try Giving Yourself Away

Remember the words of the Lord Jesus, how he said,
It is more blessed to give than to receive.

ACTS 20:35 KJV

I feel blessed to have been born to a mother who left her welcome mat on the front porch until her death at age eighty-nine. A second blessing came in the form of a husband who is a Christian, a people person, and one who loves to open the doors of our home to everyone.

He extended his first invitation shortly after we returned from our honeymoon when he invited a couple to our home. They accepted, and I learned about the invitation—in that order.

Now it wasn't as if he did not have all the facts.

Before we set the wedding date, I made certain he knew that my most outstanding kitchen skills were drying dishes and setting the table. I also made peanut butter crisscross cookies from a recipe I found in *Highlights* magazine about the time I was twelve years old. And potato salad! I could mix an excellent potato salad if the eggs and potatoes were boiled.

Not to worry, though. I decided when I heard about our guests; my new husband had already told me he knew how to cook. (It had been music to my ears!) In fact, his culinary specialty was gravy. I was pretty impressed. Mama always said it wasn't easy to make good gravy.

Our friends, the best man and matron of honor at our wedding, came to dinner. Don fried chicken, cooked rice, and made gravy. I warmed canned vegetables and burned canned biscuits. But I remember the gravy the best.

After removing the golden brown chicken from the skillet, Don added flour to the inch-deep, melted Crisco. He added more flour, and even more flour, until our two-pound bag was nearly depleted. When he was satisfied with the color of the flour, he added water, which resulted in enough light brown substance to fill the yellow Pyrex mixing bowl, the largest bowl of our new set of four. The substance was easily sliced and served atop the rice. Don called it gravy.

Sitting at that tiny wooden table covered with a damask cloth, our wedding china, and the yellow mixing bowl brimming with gravy, I realized I needed to learn to cook—quickly. So I began my long love affair with cookbooks and pots and pans. We continued inviting friends and family for dinner, but the menu rarely ever included gravy.

PRACTICAL POINTERS

In case you, too, have troubles with gravy, try this recipe:

After roasting a chicken, remove it to a platter and keep it warm. Spoon off the grease from the roasting pan, leaving the meat juices behind. You'll need about 2 cups meat juice, so if necessary add canned chicken broth. Then add:

2–4 tbsp of the poured-off grease
2–4 tbsp flour
chopped giblets or meat from the neck (optional)
$\frac{1}{4}$ cup light cream (optional)
salt and pepper to taste

Cook, stirring constantly, until gravy is as thick as
you want it to be. Immediately turn off the heat.
If you end up with lumps, strain the gravy through
a fine-mesh sieve. Serve hot.

Wedding and baby showers provided more reasons to
open doors and invite friends. Then my father died pre-
maturely, and my mother passed the family holiday
torch to me. When Don and I hosted holiday celebrations for the extended family, we sometimes found ourselves playing host and hostess to as many as twenty-five
people. We were not much more than twenty-five years
old at the time, but we enjoyed each gathering. And
when the church hostess approached me about "feeding
the preachers" during a revival meeting, I *knew* I had
reached the pinnacle of Southern Baptist hospitality.

A few years after the first preachers came to visit
and eat, I read a delightful little book entitled, *Try
Giving Yourself Away.* This little paperback spoke to my
heart. As I read, I was challenged to become an encourager to those around me, to minister to those in need,

and to open the doors of my home to others. I pondered on these simple thoughts. I liked what I had read.

Shortly thereafter we bought our first house. It was red brick with three tiny bedrooms, one ceramic tile bath, and a one-car carport. It was just an assembly of wood and glass, bricks and concrete, occupying a space called 5756 Dale Drive, in a city named Satsuma, Alabama—but it quickly became a home when the Sims family of three came to reside within the walls. We had little furniture and even less money, but we felt blessed and we wanted to share our home with others.

"Our home will likely be our single largest material asset," Don said. "God has blessed us with this house. We should use it for Him." Thus our one thousand square feet of bricks and mortar took on new meaning. We dedicated our home to God and made a commitment to use it as a place to celebrate the Good News with others.

We opened the doors and people came. No one noticed that the living room was not furnished or that we had eight chairs squeezed around our tiny table for four. Gourmet meant we were having pot roast. We spent many happy hours with family and friends crowded around that borrowed table, eating, laughing, and loving.

We invited and everyone came, and they came

back. We found it easy to give ourselves away—at home!

Fulfillment comes to the homes of Christians when we invite family, neighbors, and even strangers to come inside. Some come to laugh and to celebrate. Others come because they need a friend, someone who will listen and encourage. When hurting deeply, some just need a hug and a private place to cry.

Are you willing to offer your home as a place of celebration or a refuge for someone who is hurting? Try giving yourself away at home. You will likely discover that the blessing that comes to you is greater than the one that you gave. What a paradox!

GLIMPSES

*Giving is the secret of a healthy life. . .
not necessarily money,
but encouragement,
sympathy, and understanding.*

JOHN D. ROCKEFELLER

Be Sure Your Home Says, "Welcome, Come On In!"

Be devoted to one another in brotherly love.
Honor one another above yourselves.

Romans 12:10 NIV

Nearly forty years, three houses, and many blessings later, our doors are still open. Our most recent guests, a group of my former coworkers, came to dinner last night. As one friend stepped inside the door, she spoke seriously in a hushed voice. "I thought you were a Christian until I saw the flag in your front yard." Fearing the worst, I opened wide the front door and stepped outside.

You must first understand that we live in a typical

southern state. Football is practiced and played, talked about and analyzed 365 days every year. To say our two major universities, Alabama and Auburn, enjoy strong support from state residents is an understatement. Alabama football fascination comes in two color combinations: red and white or orange and blue.

At our house we fly purple and gold and support Louisiana State University, Don's state team. Of course, Alice was only teasing; but her statement confirmed to me how clearly one's home speaks to guests even before they enter.

The holder for our flag is permanently attached to a tree trunk. We have always used it to display the American flag on patriotic holidays. Recently yard flags have become more popular. Now we own a collection for special occasions. We think of our flag as a cheery first greeting to those who visit and others who just pass by.

Have you ever stood in the street and tried to envision your home through the eyes of a stranger? I did just that in early spring last year, and I did not like what I saw. The grass was still brown from winter. An outdated holiday flag was partially twisted around the pole with one corner struggling to wave. Every bed was flowerless and covered with weeds. The concrete front walk was leaf-stained and dirty. I was happy to see the first signs of spring, but not thrilled that those green sprigs were pushing their way up through cracks in the brick front steps. Empty white wooden planters sat on either side of the dust-covered front door. The scene was a silent testimony to a husband who travels all week and is blessed with a wife who has her own definition of the great outdoors—the distance between the back door of the house and the front door of her car.

I walked back to the street for another quick glance. Was our home sending a message? Yes, loud and clear. "Everyone has moved off and abandoned me. I'm cold, bored, and sad."

What a difference a few months can make! Without even ringing the doorbell, the approaching guest is certain a family is in residence. The now-retired husband has weeded, trimmed, sprigged, and even painted. He changes flags on a monthly basis. The wife has "planted" silk trees in the white planters by the front door and a real herb garden in the backyard. The house is vibrant again. It looks happy and loved, communicating to those who approach the front door a warm welcome, a loud and clear, "Come on in!"

Recently I met with neighbors to make plans for our subdivision's participation in Mobile by Candlelight, a citywide Christmas celebration. While getting acquainted, one neighbor asked where I lived. When I told her I lived next door to where we were meeting, she said, "Oh, you're the lady with the pretty house!"

"My house is no different from yours," I replied. "Each of us has been blessed with a pretty home."

"But you always have outside floodlights on and a dim light on your front porch. Sometimes we just drive by at night. It looks so inviting." What a compliment we received for our five-dollar investment in a dimmer switch and the minimal cost of front yard spotlights.

A friendly feeling outside promises warmth inside. When our doorbells ring and guests arrive, they deserve to be greeted promptly and warmly invited to enter.

Years ago friends came anticipating a friendly visit. I wasn't ready, nor was the food. Sensing a problem, they asked, "Did we come at the wrong time?" My frustration made them feel uncomfortable, maybe even unwelcome. On that Sunday afternoon many years ago, I promised myself that would never happen again. My hair may not be combed nor the steaks thawed, but I will open the door with a smile on my face—and perhaps an invitation—or command—to report immediately to the kitchen to help!

PRACTICAL POINTERS

Neatly trimmed yards, a freshly painted mailbox, and blooming plants say "Welcome" as guests approach any front door. Hanging pots filled with ferns, a wooden or wicker swing, outside chimes and birdhouses, squirrel feeders, even a small fountain, can display some part of the personality of those who live inside. A tidy front door area is pleasing to daytime guests and soft lighting adds warmth for night visitors who ring the doorbell or others who just walk by.

As guests come inside, welcome them with softly scented burning candles or a subtle hint of cinnamon filtering from the kitchen. Soft background music adds ambience. Dishes, even cups and saucers, on the table speak to every guest, saying, "I was expecting you. I am glad you came today."

I am sure you have your own special ways of welcoming guests. Won't you come over and share them with me? We could sit right down and visit. The temperature is dropping outside and our own tea party is waiting. We could chat and share our hospitality ideas and stories while sipping tea from brightly colored bone china mugs. Wouldn't that be fun?

This is the story I would tell you. It is one of my favorites. A friend came by to drop off some travel information she had borrowed. I wasn't home, so Lyn left the bag of books on the table beside my back door. The radio inside had inadvertently been left on, and music filtered outside to the porch through the intercom. When I returned, I had a message from Lyn. "You are the only person I know who welcomes guests with classical music, even when you aren't home!"

GLIMPSES

When I open my door,
do I send rays to dispel the night? . . .
When I open my heart, does it shine
somewhere like the flame in a cavern,
one living pinprick warding off the
monstrous cavity of nothingness?
Am I light in the world,
and is this house set on a hill
for the city to see?

KAREN MAINS,
Open Heart, Open Home

Come to My Table

So he sent two of his disciples, telling them,
"Go into the city,
and a man carrying a jar of water will meet you.
Follow him. Say to the owner of the house he enters,
'The Teacher asks: Where is my guest room,
where I may eat the Passover with my disciples?'
He will show you a large upper room,
furnished and ready.
Make preparations for us there."
MARK 14:13–15 NIV

In one of the most beautiful, yet saddest, of all New Testament stories, Jesus broke bread for the final time with the twelve He chose as disciples. Several years ago Don and I had the opportunity to step from the bright outdoor sunshine and climb the stairs to the room thought to be the one where Jesus met for the last time with the group of twelve. A room and a table suddenly overshadowed the dusty streets Jesus walked two thousand years ago, the same ones we had walked. My eyes adjusted to the semidarkness, and I saw that the stone walls surrounding me defined a large room. I remain overwhelmed even today as I consider what took place, if not in this very room, surely in one like it.

Jesus knew this would be the last time He could be with His disciples. Why did He choose this room to sit—or recline in the custom of that day—and break bread? Who was the nameless believer who opened his home to Jesus and the disciples for an evening? What impact did the encounter have on the lives of those present? And more important, what impact will the "table talks" of Jesus have on me?

Think of the lives Jesus had already touched with His "table talks." Zacchaeus became not only a gracious host but also a changed man when Jesus was a guest in his home. A specious meadow was transformed into a banquet table with loaves and fishes on the menu. And a table conversation gave way to a sacrificial gift of great value as Mary poured out her perfume—and her soul. Even after the resurrection, Jesus revealed Himself as He broke bread with the disciples from Emmaus and later prepared a breakfast complete with bread and fish for Simon Peter.

Reflecting for years on these ideas, I developed a new respect for what happens as people sit at tables. Dignitaries meet in highly protected rooms to discuss policies that affect the safety and future of every person on this planet. Leaders gather to negotiate laws for our country, while church leaders plan for outreach to the lost. Within the walls of their own homes, Christians strengthen other Christians and win nonbelievers to the faith. And most of this activity takes place around a table.

During much of my lifetime, the table was the hub of the activity in almost every home. Hungry families ate together and feelings were expressed. Mealtime was an opportunity for those who shared a home to get in touch with each other. In today's society, however, gathering at the table is almost a lost art, even for the most dedicated Christian families.

Our generation can be called a microwave society. Breakfast is nonexistent or picked up at the local fast-food restaurant. Children eat lunch at school, while working parents eat out. The designated chef for the night picks up dinner before returning home. Family members microwave individual portions to be eaten alone. And hospitality, the art of reaching outside your home and inviting others to your table, is seldom discussed and less often practiced.

Years ago I read an article describing the results of a study that focused on adults who had grown up in an impoverished crime-ridden area of our country. Many of the young lives were lost to a lifetime of crime or an untimely death. But others were successful professionals, educators, physicians, or businessmen. Somehow they beat the odds. The study found a common thread: Each successful study participant could pinpoint a place and a time when someone showed interest and took time to encourage him or her. Many had ongoing relationships with that person. Others had only had a one-time encounter with the encourager, yet that inspiration made a lifetime of difference.

God touched me in love, and I want to touch others. I want to be an encourager and make a difference in someone's life. I want to invite someone to my table.

On any given day I can think of 101 reasons why I shouldn't invite anyone. And on that day I am the loser. But today I invited someone to come to my table.

I will invite others to come. I will follow the example of the Savior, who invited the disciples to sit with Him at that eventful meal recorded in the Gospels.

PRACTICAL POINTERS

Whom will you invite to your table?
- Perhaps you know someone who is lonely. Invite them to share a bowl of soup and, more important, an afternoon with you.
- Almost everyone has a friend who is hurting. Call this person and say, "Come for tea (or coffee). We can visit for a while."
- Minister to a friend who has experienced disappointment.
- Invite friends to an "old-fashioned Sunday dinner."
- Celebrate the birthday of the oldest member of your extended family.

Reclaim your table. Sit with family members, friends,

acquaintances, and even strangers. Who can measure the impact that, through Christ, we can have on the lives of others? It is time for Christians to slow down, sit down, be encouragers, and get in touch with others—around a table.

GLIMPSES

A meal is an experience not only of biological food but also of emotional, physiological, intellectual, and spiritual food: sustenance.

ROBERT FABING

Tea for Two–or More

Charge them that are rich in this world,
that they be not highminded,
nor trust in uncertain riches,
but in the living God,
who giveth us richly all things to enjoy;
That they do good, that they be rich in good works.
1 TIMOTHY 6:17–18 KJV

Invite a friend for tea. You won't need to plan a menu, go to the grocery store, or clean your oven. Use your friendliest teapot. Pour hot tea into dainty cups covered with bright flowers or cheerful earthenware mugs. Or serve iced tea in a frosted glass complete with a thin slice of lemon on the rim. (In the South we serve iced tea year-round.) It's not all about tea. Rather, it's about reaching out in love—about inviting someone to your table.

The English gave us this idea of afternoon tea. Delicate ladies sometimes grew faint and needed a little nourishment to tide them over until the dinner hour. They made tea in the afternoon, added a few "biscuits" (known to us as "cookies") or dainty cakes—and invited friends. A Devonshire tea usually included scones or crumpets, a rather flat, non-sweet bread.

If you don't like tea, you could still come to my house. We will mix some punch. Sometimes the English ladies served chilled beverages from miniature crystal punch bowls on hot summer days. It's not the tea that makes the gathering special. But something happens when women gather at tea tables.

Recently I called a friend. We chatted for a while. I told her she was on my mind and on my heart. She is special, a strong Christian, but life has not been easy for her, and her losses have been tremendous. When I expressed my concern, she began to cry and accepted my invitation to come to my house for tea.

I found some dainty paper napkins and colorful china mugs for the two of us. I turned on soft music and wished for a plate of warm tea cakes. All I had was left-over chocolate chip cookies, so I made some tea and waited for her arrival.

She was gracious as usual, thanked me for calling and for inviting. We talked about grandchildren and even laughed a little. Even when laughing, though, her eyes revealed her hurt. We cried and talked about her loss. She hugged me as she left and said she felt better. I think that she did. Something good happened that afternoon—even though the tea and cookies were left untouched.

You may want to plan a happy gathering for a group of young women from your church or neighborhood. Invite them to come while the children are in school—a great time for some adult conversation and a break from sorting laundry. Pamper them with tea, punch, and goodies.

Or, if *you* are a young woman, invite a group of seniors from your church to a late morning tea. Mail dainty invitations and follow up with a call to be certain your guests have transportation and directions. Pick up a vase of silk flowers, get out the bone china cups, and set out your best napkins. Polish your silver trays and fill them with small sandwiches and homemade cookies (slice and bake if you don't have time for "from scratch").

A dear friend shared with me her version of

afternoon tea for seniors. She had observed widows in her neighborhood as they left for church on Sunday morning dressed in their finest. Many spent Sunday afternoons at home alone, still dressed in their church attire. Hilda's idea was to invite the neighborhood ladies to her home one Sunday of every month for tea and a time of fellowship. She called me a second time to discuss this Sunday afternoon tea idea. In her characteristic straightforward manner she said, "I always thought about doing that, but I never have. Maybe someone who reads your book will do it. I want you to put this in your book."

Will you use my friend's suggestion and invite the ladies of your neighborhood for tea and crumpets? Perhaps, a one-time affair or a Spring Tea each year about Eastertime. Serve the tea outside while listening to taped classical music. Or plan a birthday tea in honor of your senior neighborhood friend.

Irene, a lifelong friend of my mother, continues to spend holidays with our extended family. As we celebrated one occasion, Irene admitted she was approaching her eightieth birthday and added, "I have never had a birthday party." She explained that she grew up in the country with many siblings and without the luxury of birthday celebrations. Widowed now, with no children, she had never been honored on her special day. I thought about this for just one moment and I knew. We were going to have a *big* tea party.

My cousin Pat and I planned a pink and lacy party. We invited Irene's family, her church family, and her neighbors. A parade of seniors arrived on that Sunday afternoon, decked out in every shade of pastel, holding exquisitely wrapped packages in their white-gloved hands. Each registered their attendance in the guest book, a permanent reminder of a happy occasion. Friends chatted as they ate tiny sandwiches and cakes while sipping punch. Southern women are akin, at least in habit, to the British.

We gathered to honor a woman who had taken part in many celebrations for others but had never been honored herself. It was a beautiful experience for each of us. Irene was delighted, and the guests enjoyed the afternoon. But Pat and I received the greatest blessing as we saw a childlike look of excitement in the eyes of an eighty-year-old woman encircled by loving friends.

You could plan a tea party for someone turning eighty. Or a "Senior Tea" and encourage the ladies to wear pretty straw hats and white gloves. Or plan a birthday tea for your daughter or a granddaughter turning eight.

Buy inexpensive straw hats, silk flowers, ribbon, and lace. Help each little guest decorate her own special hat.

Whether expecting a large group or just one friend, I look forward with anticipation to tea. And sometimes I have a tea party all by myself.

For ten years Don traveled weekly to distant cities. On dreary winter evenings I returned home after work to a cold, unfriendly house. Sometimes I warmed a cup of tea in the microwave, turned up the thermostat, and curled up on the couch with a book. It wasn't the best tea party ever, but much warmer than the "pity party" I could have planned. Just a colorful paper napkin, bone china mug, and tea. But I felt a little warmer inside, much like your guests will feel when they come to your house for tea.

Whom will you invite to your table for tea? A new neighbor? A long-ago classmate? A lonely single-again? Your pastor's wife? Invite someone. It will be a double blessing—a blessing to your guest and a blessing to you. You may not change the course of the world by opening the doors of your home for tea—but you will touch the lives of those who enter. They, in turn, will touch others—and together we *can* make a difference.

PRACTICAL POINTERS

This recipe for berry muffins is an excellent addition to any tea party:

2 eggs

½ cup milk

¼ cup (½ stick) melted butter

2 cups flour

1 tbsp baking powder

½ tsp salt

½ cup sugar

1 cup blueberries, raspberries, or other berries

Preheat oven to 400 degrees. Insert 24 paper cupcake holders in 2-inch muffin tins. Beat eggs until foamy; then stir in milk and butter. Sift dry ingredients and fold into wet mixture, stirring just enough to blend (do not overmix). Gently fold the berries into batter. Pour batter into muffin tins and bake for 12 minutes or until muffins are lightly browned. Cool for a few minutes, then turn out onto a wire rack. Serve warm. Makes 2 dozen muffins. Make double and freeze a batch to have on hand.

GLIMPSES

The first cup of tea
moistens my lips and throat;
the second cup breaks my loneliness.

LU T'UNG

Hospitality on
a Shoestring Budget

"[God] never left himself without a witness;
there were always his reminders—
the kind things he did such as. . .
giving you food and gladness."

ACTS 14:17 TLB

All this fuss about opening doors, inviting people, and making tea might sound interesting to you. *But not anytime soon,* you think as you read. *Maybe later. Certainly not now—not at this stage in my life. I simply don't have the time or the money.*

In reality, each of us has the same amount of time —twenty-four hours each day. We can long for, hope for, and pray for a twenty-fifth hour, and it does happen. But only once each year on that wonderful Saturday night in

October (my favorite day of the year) when we turn our clocks back before we go to bed. Finally, I have a day with twenty-five hours. I savor every moment of it.

Each of us has "time," and each of us has the same amount. We have 24 hours, 1,440 minutes, or 86,400 seconds each day. How we choose to use our time differs widely from one person to another. If hospitality is important to you, you will want to regularly invest some of your time reaching out to others.

While we may admit that each of us has the same amount of time, we still choose to hide behind our stretched budgets to avoid opening our hearts and homes. But just as we make choices about time, each of us makes choices about what we do with our money. Some families who have limited finances find opportunities for hospitality and fun with a minimal price tag. Our children grew up in a home where entertaining on a budget was a way of life. They did not know there was another way to provide hospitality. With one income, both parents in college, and two children in private school, we planned our first *formal* dinner party (using the word "formal" loosely).

It was the Christmas season when we invited four of Don's coworkers and their spouses to our home for dinner. I was a full-time student with *no* extra time and even less extra money. To make this venture work, I had to be very creative. So I served simple low-budget meals to my family for several weeks, saved a few dollars, and bought a large ham. The day of the party, I added a congealed salad, vegetables, and yeast rolls made from my grandmother's recipe. A homemade-from-scratch pound cake was the only dessert choice.

The table was set with our wedding china and our best silver, 1847 Rogers Silverplate. Colorful paper napkins (purchased for half of the original price) and place cards made by the children added color to the dining table. We played Christmas music (*both* albums) on the stereo turntable. Guests who crossed the threshold of our home that evening never knew they were entertained *without* a budget!

Shortly after moving our membership to a new church, Don and I planned a party for a group of twelve couples. We called it "Music and Mixers," an easy way to host a large group on a small budget. You can have a similar party by making or buying invitations with a musical theme. Include the following information: "Please select a song title. Bring props or wear clothing to depict the song title you have chosen. After dinner, other guests will attempt to guess *your* title." At our party one couple depicted a popular song from the forties, "Red Roses for a Blue Lady." The wife wore blue and the husband presented her with three long-stemmed red roses, later given to the hostess as a gift. After dinner, assemble the group in your largest area for "The Most Creative Song Title" contest. When each couple or guest has presented their mystery song title, the group nominates three (or more) of the most creative presentations, then votes by secret ballot on the winner. A tape or an inexpensive CD is a likely prize. At our house a short devotional based on Scriptures related to music was an inspirational ending to a fun party. To get ready for this party, decorate with sheet music, albums, and eight-track tapes. Choose appropriate music for your guests' listening pleasure, such as fifties, country, or classical. Placing tapes or CD players in several rooms allows for choices and draws people with similar tastes together to visit.

We learned early that we couldn't buy everything we thought we needed for entertaining. So we chose to use creatively what we did have and focus on guests rather than things. You, too, can use what you have as you open your home to others while still living within your shoestring budget.

PRACTICAL POINTERS

Ideas for low-cost hospitality:

- Drag out the leisure suit, miniskirts, and bell-bottoms for a "Seventies Gathering." Locate those old hiking boots to wear with your shorts or your out-of-style polyester suit with white socks and heels, then mail unstylish invitations to a "Tacky Party."
- Or use old luggage, maps, oversized sunglasses, and cameras to decorate for your "Getaway Celebration," while you display outdated travel magazines from local agencies. T-shirts you have collected from obscure places will add to the décor, and you may want to save the most outlandish shirt to wrap and give to your guest that wins (by secret ballot) the prestigious "Best Dressed Tourist" award. Greet each guest at the door with a fake plane ticket. At meal-time direct them to pick up their food—brown bag lunches served airline style.
- Serve your guests at a "Salad and Hot Food Bar Restaurant." Plan the salads yourself and set up the salad bar on a long cabinet. Ask each guest, or couple, to bring a casserole for

the hot bar. Hang a sign naming your restaurant, perhaps a takeoff on your own local chain restaurant. Take orders for drinks and serve them to your guests at their tables.

- If you travel with a group, afterward plan a "Picture Party." Begin preparation even as you travel by purchasing napkins or inexpensive items for favors. These will delight fellow travelers as they relive a moment of the trip. Use travel posters and memorabilia for decorations and food ideas from the area that you visited. After an inexpensive soup and salad meal, the group can share personal photos.

- While in graduate school, our married children planned parties with their fellow students. Each brought food and a copy of their wedding video. New friends shared laughter, tears, and wedding memories. You, too, can invite your friends to bring their videos or wedding albums, as well as one item that was served at their wedding reception. A small homemade sheet cake and punch prepared by the host complete the menu for a light meal before or after "the weddings." Select one couple, perhaps the couple who has been married the longest, to be showered with rice (or birdseed) as they leave. Showers of rice will likely bring back fond memories and provide an enjoyable grand finale for your "Re-Wedding Party."

- Chinese New Year is another fun time for a celebration. Invite friends or couples for a Chinese dinner. Let your guests know you are providing soup, egg rolls, and fortune cookies. With or without a planned menu, ask each to pick up one entree from their favorite Chinese restaurant. Display the food Chinese buffet style. Inexpensive chopsticks provide dinner-time entertainment. Sharing "fortunes" will likely lead to a few laughs. The host might close the evening by expressing his "good fortune" in having friends to come for fun and fellowship.

- Open your home to a group of your friends who sing and/or play musical instruments for "A Night of Music." Plan for audience participation after renditions by the musicians. Printed sheets with the words of old-time favorites such as "Pack Up Your Troubles," "Daisy, Daisy," and "Row Your Boat" sung in rounds will bring back fond memories to any older group. Honor the musicians with a dessert party to close the evening. Use napkins with a musical motif and serve chocolate cake with coffee or tea. Token musical favors, perhaps a kazoo or written thank-yous for each musician, become tangible reminders of this night of fun.

- When weather permits, plan an outside "Good Neighbor Party." Send a written note to the people in your neighborhood you have not met. Invite them to drop by one Saturday morning for coffee and doughnuts. Include in the invitation envelope a tiny Ziploc bag filled with a teaspoon of sugar. Decorate your outside area with ladders, rakes, shovels, and other inside/outside gadgets neighbors sometimes need to borrow. Use sugar as a centerpiece on the food table—an opened five-pound bag and the proverbial "cup of sugar" good neighbors always borrow.

- Or plan a Sunday afternoon ice cream supper on the patio. Ask neighbors to bring their favorite flavor of ice cream. Invite newer neighbors as guests. Set up outside games for the children and a circle of lawn chairs for adults—a place to gather for fellowship.

- Another idea is for the host to provide the entrée while guests bring "potluck." Number your plates on the underside. Use corresponding numbers on place cards. Rather than names, each guest finds his or her appropriate place by matching numbers on plates with place cards randomly assigned.

GLIMPSES
*If there's any at all,
there is enough to share.*
ELIZABETH MULLENDORE

Life After Dust

Man shall not live by bread alone.

MATTHEW 4:4 KJV

Every week, my family ate Saturday night supper at my mother's house. One Saturday night, while she and I were cleaning up the kitchen, I noticed a piece of Mama's wedding china in the kitchen cabinet. I gingerly lifted the dusty covered vegetable bowl from the back corner and placed it on the tiled floor in front of me. I hoped to recapture a childhood memory.

As a child I was intrigued with the delicate white china covered with multicolored flowers and strange words printed on the underside. Now, I turned the dusty bowl upside down and found that the name of the German manufacturer was obscured by masking tape. One word, "Whatley," hand-printed by Mama with a black marker, identified the bowl's owner.

The bewildered look on my face did not escape Mama, but she thought her explanation plausible. "Mr. Turner died, and I took a bowl of fresh peas when the church provided food the day of the funeral."

I could not believe what I had heard. "Your bowl might have been broken or it could have been misplaced," I quietly protested. "That bowl is important to me. It is filled with thousands of memories from my past."

I was still sitting on the yellow and green tiled floor gazing at the bowl when she finally spoke. "Take the bowl home with you tonight. But I want you to promise me that you will use it. Take the platter also, and use both of them when you have company."

The china had lost most of its meaning to Mama years earlier on the night Daddy died. I reluctantly, yet gratefully, agreed to take the dishes to my house and use them. I promised Mama they would never gather dust again. And I also knew that they would never find themselves on another unfamiliar table. I suppose I had finally reached the age of accountability, the age when one recognizes the meaning of "family treasure."

Later I realized Mama had given me other treasures over the years. Once she brought a brass bell to our house. She told me it was the bell her mother used more than seventy-five years earlier to call her children to their table at mealtime. I cleaned the bell and began using it to call the extended family to my dining room for holiday meals. A white ceramic soup tureen and platter, hand-made by Mama for me one Christmas, lost its shelf life. It became a serving bowl filled with gumbo, soup, even chicken and dumplings, to serve family and friends.

I emptied the dusty plastic grapes from my grand-mother's antique berry bowl and filled it with fresh fruit salad for my guests. Poppy seed dressing for the salad was spooned from her hundred-year-old sugar bowl.

One piece of masking tape taught me a valuable lesson. Rather than simply displaying dishes and other special items, we should lovingly use them on our own tables. This is one way to say to your guests, "You are special!"

Please accompany me now as we take a quick trip through my house. I need your help. We are look-ing for other dusty objects that need a new life in the world of hospitality.

Three or four gift books tied together with wide gold ribbon, complete with bow, becomes a "package" to adorn a tea table or other serving table. A small piece of framed handwork displayed on an easel adds a whimsi-cal touch when placed next to a teapot.

Next, pick up small crystal or ceramic vases as we move from room to room. No need for them to match: Variety in vases, like variety in friends, will add spice to my luncheon. I will fill the vases with water and add pansies. If fresh flowers are not available, a sprig of greenery is a special touch that speaks an individual wel-come to each guest.

Have you spotted the pottery pieces I purchased while traveling? The small earthenware pitcher makes an interesting syrup vessel when serving waffles. Larger pottery items become containers for pots of mums or ivy for a casual lunch or dinner. Or combine pretty paper products with pottery for an easy cleanup after Saturday morning brunch.

Pitchers of every type are just waiting to be used: small crystal pitchers for cream for coffee; tiny silver pitchers for salad dressing; little china pitchers for lemon juice for iced tea.

As we walk through the kitchen door, you imme-diately eye the copper collection hanging above the kitchen cabinets gathering dust. I know you are catching the idea when you ask if they are ever retrieved, dusted, and used. Right! The copper colander—and also my enamel, stainless steel, and even my old plastic colander—all double as luncheon centerpieces when filled with colorful fruit and raw vegetables. Other pieces of copper are also used for centerpieces and for serving food.

The tiny glass Bluebird of Happiness is a favorite of mine. I am delighted when you notice it and the other glass birds as we move from room to room. A collection of birds nesting on a leafy tree branch creates a unique tablescape for a spring or summer luncheon. Add a small birdhouse or bird feeder for even more interesting conversation. Place cards declaring "Birds of a Feather Flock Together" continue the theme, and taped bird sounds playing softly in the background complete a perfect outside-inside atmosphere.

You may be thinking, "But I don't have any birds, copper, pottery, or crystal." Perhaps you don't. And I don't have many of the pretty things that live at your house. We cannot use what we do not have, but we can learn to use what we do have. Use your dust catchers creatively.

PRACTICAL POINTERS

Mark your page, close this book, and lay it aside. Yes, you did read the sentence correctly. I want you to grab a notepad and pen, attach your creative thinking cap securely, and take a walk-through tour of your home. Now is the time for you to become intimately acquainted with your dust catchers. Your bric-a-brac can have a new life with just a little help from you.

A beloved Easter basket from bygone years becomes a sewing basket when friends who sew come to lunch. Fill the basket with fabric, thread, scissors, a tape measure, and other sewing items. Or fill the same basket with booties and knitting thread for a baby shower centerpiece. Gather all the candlesticks in your home and place them on a mirror in the center of the table for a lovely birthday or New Year's Eve celebration. Dig out your old college blankets and football jerseys. Invite friends to watch the big game dressed in their favorite jersey or team colors. Make a pot of chili and have an inside tailgate party.

Since I retired, a group of former coworkers gather at my house once a month for dinner (which they provide). For several months I planned simple theme table decorations. Then one particularly busy day I did not give the dining table a thought until an hour prior to their arrival time. I quickly attempted to transform my Victorian dining room into a street scene in Venice. I found a worn checked tablecloth in an upstairs linen closet, then pulled out white dishes and an assortment of mismatched candles. A basket lined with a colorful kitchen towel held packaged pasta and Italian sauce in jars; it soon became a conversation centerpiece. I scattered an eight-ounce bag of dry pasta among the plates and lit the candles just before the first guest arrived. We ate lasagna by candlelight beneath my largest umbrella, which I had attached to the chandelier. Instant Italian pizzeria!

Think creatively. Once I used a long mirror in the center of my dining room table. I placed a small ceramic cruise ship on the mirror and built Greek Islands from dirt covered with rocks found in my backyard. Just before my guests arrived for dinner, I poured a small amount of water around the ship, carefully avoiding the mounds of dirt. If a mirror placed in the middle of the dining room table can become the Aegean Sea, just think what magical objects are nesting at your house waiting to be of service.

Check out every decorative item, serving piece, and all that "stuff" packed in the back of closets and in the attic. Then on a moment's notice you can bring some dusty relics to life again in a new role as you welcome people into your home.

GLIMPSES
*Employ whatever God has
entrusted you with,
in doing good,
all possible good,
in every possible kind and degree. . . .*

JOHN WESLEY

Lists, Lists, Lists

Be kindly affectioned one to another with brotherly love;
in honour preferring one another;
Not slothful in business;
fervent in spirit; serving the Lord.
ROMANS 12:10–11 KJV

I make lists of things to do today and things to do later. I make grocery shopping lists and lists of people to call. Sometimes I lose a list and I panic. At that moment my ever-helpful husband tells me that, perhaps, I make too many lists. Nevertheless, when I have a written reminder, I am certain I accomplish more of what is truly important to me. And because opening my heart and my home to others is important, I always have hospitality lists.

My "Things to Buy for Hospitality" list is with me when I shop, and it goes in my luggage when I travel. On the list are functional and decorative items I need or would enjoy using. The list is also helpful to family members who would like a gift idea. Our children and grandchildren have given me books with instructions on folding napkins and creating elaborate tablescapes. On special occasions I have received place card holders, napkins, and napkin rings. One creative gift included menus, recipes, and CDs for dining background music. A recent Christmas gift from our sixteen-year-old granddaughter was a box of exquisite gold and white party invitations. My last birthday gift from Don was a lace tablecloth for the dining table. (Now we can entertain again without using a large mirror to cover the hole in the old cloth.) Many of these items came from my list. Hostesses, whether budding or seasoned, welcome gifts that can be used for entertaining.

PRACTICAL POINTERS

Let me suggest that you get a pen and paper and begin your "Things to Buy for Hospitality" list. Include those items that you never remember to buy. Do you need new green napkins, fourteen-inch tapers, or twelve-inch paper doilies? A new tea pitcher or a large gumbo pot? Use your list as a bookmark as you continue to read. Keep your pen handy; you will likely need it.

Seasonal items such as pastel place mats and rabbit napkin rings, American flags, fall centerpieces, and Christmas decorations are often found on clearance tables at greatly reduced prices. I may not have many Irish genes, but if I am lucky and find St. Patrick's Day decorations for a fraction of the original price, you can be sure I will have a theme party next March.

Dishes are one of my many weaknesses. During our forty-plus years of marriage, my collections of china and crystal have outgrown cabinets, china cabinets, and larger china cabinets. Many of the items stored on those shelves were gifts. Others were purchased at estate or garage sales where silver, china, crystal, and bric-a-brac can be found at ridiculously low prices. It still amazes me that families sell their heirlooms for twenty-five cents each.

On a recent trip to Jackson Hole, Wyoming, I browsed through an upscale gift shop and landed upstairs in the midst of the 75% off merchandise. My kind of sale! And I saw dishes, not ordinary dishes, but *blue and white* dishes. *I shouldn't*. . .but I did—to the tune of four place settings. I just could not resist. The cost of the dishes was minimal. (Unfortunately, the cost of the mailing is another story.)

"Napkins" is a standard entry on any hospitality list. I dig to the bottom of every napkin bin that is topped with a sign that reads "Sale." With no regard to the month or the season, I buy an assortment. If the sale is after Christmas and the napkins are red, I just think Valentine's Day or the Fourth of July.

For hard-to-find items on my list, I sometimes resort to mail-order catalogs with good results. After searching our city for individual salt and pepper shakers without any success, a friend suggested I might find them in a mail-order catalog. I found what I wanted, ordered by telephone, and they arrived on my doorstep just a few days later.

But I have another and far more important hospitality list. This list is always written in my current calendar. We call it our "People List." For years when we crossed paths with old friends, someone always said with great sincerity: "We need to get together!" But we never called, nor did they. We encountered the same people months later (or even years later) and had the same conversation. Other times, Don and I would discuss inviting newcomers to our church, young married couples, or friends who were lonely. Too often we, like the baby cub I described in an earlier chapter, did more talking than walking.

But years ago we decided that anytime we mentioned inviting anyone, the name would be added to our "People List." Now when we open our calendar, we see the names in writing and the faces in our hearts. It may take months to make the hospitality event happen. Sometimes we even have to transfer names from one calendar to another. But a name is not removed until doors are opened and guests are welcomed.

Did you cross paths with old friends recently and talk about getting together? Have you noticed a moving van unloading on your street? Does the name of a coworker come to mind? Who will be first on *your* "People List"?

GLIMPSES
"Love they neighbor"
is a precept which could transform the
world if it were universally practiced.

MARY MCLEOD BETHUNE

Pampering Overnight Guests

Keep on loving each other. . . .
Do not forget to entertain strangers,
for by so doing some people have
entertained angels without knowing it.

HEBREWS 13:1–2 NIV

Often our grown sons reminisce about guests who came to visit when they were just children. Their conversation always includes a favorite aunt.

Aunt Alice, Don's mother's sister, was diminutive in size but full of energy. An early riser, every morning she would bounce into the kitchen and greet us with a cheery "Gooooood morning!" Our boys were impressed. Born to a mother who only functions after her second cup of coffee, they were not accustomed to females who talked in the early A.M. As youngsters and a few times after they were adults, each one tried to mimic her songlike rendition of "Gooooood morning!" No one ever even came close. She was special—one of a kind—the perfect houseguest.

Summer driving trips from Aunt Alice's home in Shreveport, Louisiana, to ours in Mobile, Alabama, ended about the time Aunt Alice turned eighty (but not before she accumulated a stack of speeding tickets). We invited her to return for what we knew would likely be her last visit to our home. When I made a brief stop in Shreveport, she met me for coffee to discuss the details.

"Don wants to give you a free ticket to fly to Mobile," I told her. "Will you come?"

Without hesitation she nodded and then asked, "And will it be free for me to fly back home, too?"

I smiled and assured her it would be. The date was picked and plans were made.

In preparation for her visit, I climbed the stairs one cold February night to sleep in one of our guest bedrooms. I chose for Aunt Alice's visit the room with family pictures and handwork displayed on the wall. I stopped and glanced inside before entering. "This room needs some work," I mused. Another quick look at the room across the hall where Don's sister Doris would be staying and I knew I'd best get busy. I wrote on the notepad I carried: "Vacuum, dust, tidy bathroom, and check supplies."

Magazines were outdated. The lamp beside the bed had a forty-watt bulb, inadequate for eighty-plus-year-old eyes. Large bars of white soap needed replacing with small dainty pink ones. I made a mental note to look for the new lacy hand towels I had purchased earlier.

The sheets were clean, but they did not smell fresh when I climbed into the bed. No cheerful ticktock marked the time and the sound of silence was too loud. After spending the night in my own guest bedroom, I knew what needed to be done.

Soon each bed was carefully remade and dressed in fresh linens, the very best we owned. Brighter bulbs burned in the lamps and a white wicker basket over-flowed with current magazines. Notepad and pen, alarm clock, and an inspirational book reposed on the freshly dusted night tables. On the arrival date I purchased an inexpensive bouquet of fresh flowers, added greenery from my yard, and made a colorful arrangement for each bedroom. Nothing sends a stronger message of welcome and love to guests than flowers.

Aunt Alice and Doris were almost as delighted with their rooms as we were to have them in our home. After dinner I slipped upstairs, turned down the sheets, and left a mint on the pillow of each guest. Finding bookmarks from Israel on their breakfast plates the next morning brought smiles to their faces. They felt welcomed and special.

Extra touches to normal guest preparation make a difference. With little planning and less effort (and even less money), you can pamper *your* guests. Place a small tape player in your guest bedroom and fill a basket with tapes your guests might enjoy. For early risers and coffee drinkers, leave a tray outside the door with a carafe of coffee, cream and sugar, a cup, and a pretty napkin. Add a morning newspaper or a warm muffin. Or serve your guests on a silver tray using linen napkins and bone china cups. Just a tap on the door followed by "Good morning —room service!" will delight anyone who comes to stay overnight.

That last visit with Aunt Alice was memorable. Even though a rainy weekend was predicted, skies turned blue and Mobile's colorful azaleas reached their peak just in time to welcome our visitors to the city.

Aunt Alice told stories into the night about starting "normal school" when she was fifteen, teaching school before her seventeenth birthday, and earning her undergraduate and graduate degrees. She delighted in telling us about the Bible courses that she continued to take at a nearby college until she was well into her eighties.

Each night I turned down the covers of her bed and placed a mint on her pillow. And each morning there was a special treat on her breakfast plate. In precious Aunt Alice style, she announced on that last morning, "I am not sure I will leave today, for if I do, I will never know what might have been on my breakfast plate tomorrow morning!"

Open your home. Pamper your guests. Make every overnight guest a VIP. The VIP treatment makes anyone feel special—and you'll create a memory that each of you will cherish.

Practical Pointers

Ways to pamper your guests:

- Place a box of mints on the bedside table or a chocolate chip cookie on the pillow.

- Put a "Happy" beside the plate at mealtime or even on the plate. (In our house, a "Happy" is an inexpensive item that brings joy to the recipient.)
- Pack a bag of snacks for the return trip.

GLIMPSES

*Happy is
the house that shelters a friend.*

RALPH WALDO EMERSON

Hospitality on Wheels

Offer hospitality to one another without grumbling.
Each one should use whatever gift
he has received to serve others,
faithfully administering God's grace
in its various forms.

1 Peter 4:9–10 NIV

A recently retired Nova Scotian couple crossed the Canadian border and traveled south through the United States to visit with relatives in Mobile, Alabama. Arriving in Mobile during peak afternoon traffic, they missed their turn onto Bel Air Boulevard and suddenly realized they were lost in an unfamiliar city.

Searching for a telephone or someone who might direct them to South Louise Street, the couple pulled into the parking lot of a fast-food restaurant. A woman and young man were eating in a car in the parking lot. As the travelers passed this car, they realized the young woman was crying. Rather than asking for directions, the couple asked if she needed help.

The mother assured the visitors that she and the young man, her son, were okay but having a difficult day. She had recently lost an older son in a widely publicized traffic accident in the Mobile area. Today had been a particularly bad day. The mother and son had decided to leave home for a while and were eating their evening meal in the car. Upon hearing this story, strangers from another country spoke words of comfort to the hurting mother and her son.

When the mother learned the couple had stopped to seek directions, she insisted on calling the travelers' relative to get directions from the restaurant to the relative's home. The mother said to the visitors, "You follow me, and I will take you to this address. It will be easier for me to take you than for you to find the house by yourself." She was willing to reach out to others who needed help, even as she was hurting. In doing so, she provided hospitality on wheels to visitors thousands of miles from their home.

Our twentieth-century invention, the automobile,

is often viewed as a detriment to hospitality. We sometimes think we "meet ourselves coming back" as we hurry in our cars from task to task. Some feel that we now have so many places to go that we don't slow down long enough to gather, to visit, and to fellowship. However that same automobile can provide us with unique opportunities to reach out to others in love.

Cynthia transports Christmas dinner to the nursing home where her mother resides after a debilitating stroke. The facility provides a room for the family to observe the Christmas season with their mother by having their traditional family Christmas dinner together. Turkey and all the trimmings are packed into the trunk of Cynthia's car. "It's a real trip," she says, "packing all that food, plus cakes and pies, the drinks, and everything. But I wouldn't have it any other way. Mother can't come to my house, but we can be together as a family this way." What a beautiful example of a daughter providing hospitality—on wheels!

Frequent trips to her nearby supermarket sparked a friendship between Betty and a friendly young man who worked in the produce department. One afternoon he seemed a little despondent. The young man shared that he was trying to buy a new house for his family but had been unable to sell their present home. Betty purchased fresh blueberries, returned home, and made her special blueberry pie. Then she delivered the pie to a friend, the one who worked in the produce department at her supermarket.

Elinor planned a special birthday celebration for her aunt. She invited her aunt's friends and ordered a chocolate birthday cake with pink and white icing. On the special day, she picked up the cake, napkins, flowers, and balloons, transporting hospitality to a nursing home to honor someone she loved.

My mother was hospitalized for an extended period of time following her third heart attack. Most of that eight weeks I spent at the hospital. Friends planned for Don and me to come to their home to eat on a Saturday afternoon. I was at home resting before our dinner date when I received an urgent call to return to the hospital. We kept in touch with our friends by telephone all afternoon. The crisis passed, yet I was reluctant to leave the hospital. The two couples arrived unannounced at the waiting room with a thermos of gumbo for each of us, crackers, iced tea, and dessert. The original hospitality plan didn't work; Plan B, using wheels, was more successful.

Each of us has carried food to someone during a time of crisis, an illness, or death. A unique and special way to package the food was shared with me recently. When shopping, my creative friend checks out the discounted and discontinued china patterns on sale tables. She purchases attractive single plates, one-of-a-kind china pieces, to keep in her cabinet. She calls these her "funeral dishes," giveaways to be filled with food and taken to friends in time of sickness, etc. No deposit—no return. (And much nicer than disposable.) The china becomes a permanent reminder of the creativity and thoughtfulness of a friend.

A ladies' Sunday school class at First Baptist Church, Gulf Shores, Alabama, began a Casserole Ministry patterned after a ministry of a church in another state. A supply of prepared food is stored at the church in a freezer that was purchased with donations from Sunday school classes throughout the church. Casseroles are prepared by church members and delivered to the church, labeled with the date the casserole was prepared, directions for cooking, and ingredients. Supplies of prepared food are then available for delivery to those who are ill, returning home from a hospital stay, or have other needs, whether or not they are members of First

Baptist Church. The church is often contacted if there is a need in the church or the community for a prepared meal. Class members make note of listings in "Heart Flow," a weekly church update of members who are ill or who have experienced a death in their family. When the food supply is low, a notice requesting replenishments is placed in the church newsletter. Other women contact Bettye, who heads the ministry, to offer casseroles when needed. One church member provides most of the cakes, which are freshly baked as the need arises.

This ministry has been expanded to include a meal for new members to the church. Using casseroles as an outreach tool, a meal was taken to the home of a young family who moved to Gulf Shores and visited First Baptist Church. Shortly after their first-time visit to the church, the mother gave birth to a child. The church delivered a casserole meal to the surprised (and grateful) family; as you might expect, they chose this church as their church home.

When Kathleen (a longtime participant in the ministry) and her husband returned home after an out-of-state hospital stay, they became the recipients of a casserole meal. Kathleen explained, "Until I experienced the blessing of this ministry personally, I did not fully understand the impact it has on the lives of those who receive food. And now I know it is not so much about receiving food as it is about feeling loved."

PRACTICAL POINTERS

Hospitality on wheels is a simple concept. Many ways of reaching out to others involve transportation.

- Offer to take a widow to a doctor appointment after her cataract surgery.
- Pick up groceries for a shut-in.
- Consider carpooling children for a mother who is ill.
- Offer to take neighborhood children to church.
- Invite someone who doesn't drive at night to accompany you to your church Christmas program.
- Link with your local Meals-on-Wheels delivery service for shut-ins.
- Get you own mental wheels turning to think of other ways of reaching out.

Twenty years ago Don and I had a unique opportunity to provide hospitality on wheels to three children. I crossed paths with these children at the request of an astute teacher when the youngest child slept through her class each day. The child was not completing his work; the teacher also felt there might be some problem in the home. When I met with the father, he told me this story:

The mother of his children deserted them when the youngest was an infant. The state took custody and he had fought for seven years to get the court to return the children to him. He had recently been awarded custody of the three children. Soon thereafter, however, his longtime employer declared bankruptcy, and the only new job he could find involved janitorial work at night. He took the children with him to work, bedded them down on a floor (with little sleep), and sent them to school each day. He was doing his best. Fearing he might lose custody of the children he had fought for for so long, he was reluctant to accept help from a stranger.

The next Christmas he finally agreed to allow our church to help. A Sunday school class provided gifts for the children. The father slowly learned to trust Don and me. He allowed us to take all three children, ages six, eight, and nine, to places they had never been: their first movie, first trip to McDonalds, a pizza buffet, and a restaurant to learn to order from a menu. We picked them up for Sunday school each Sunday morning. Hospitality on wheels made a difference in the lives of these children as they were exposed to truth. We saw each of them come to know Christ as their Savior. Simple acts of kindness, a dose of hospitality, and wheels taking them places they had never been touched those children—but perhaps what was touched most deeply were the lives of the two adults who drove the car.

GLIMPSES

If a true friend finds you are in need,
he or she will find a way to help.

CHARLES SWINDOLL

Outings That Say, "I Love You"

*You provide delicious food for me
in the presence of my enemies.
You have welcomed me as your guest;
blessings overflow!*

PSALM 23:5 TLB

The August morning was hot and sultry. I had hoped for a cooler day, but can one disappoint two dear women, each past her eighty-sixth birthday? The widowed sisters, Rosalie and Nellie, are my father's first cousins.

Many of my childhood memories include Rosalie. She and her husband, Joe, lived two doors down from us, and they often came over to sit on our screened front porch on hot summer nights. Mama served lemonade or homemade peach ice cream left over from Sunday.

More than fifty years have passed, and now Rosalie and I enjoy a day outing each summer. "Can we go home this year? I want to go home one more time," Rosalie said as we planned our day trip.

"Home?" I asked.

"Grand Bay—where I grew up—the land your great-grandfather homesteaded. And can we take Nellie?" Nellie is Rosalie's older sister, ninety-two years old.

So this morning I recalled my promise, disregarded the morning heat, and picked up the sisters. They were excited! They were going home.

As we sped down the hot, tree-lined country road, my mind raced faster than my car. I mentally calculated how I might make this a safe and fun day. Prior outings with Rosalie were on more familiar territory with only one hand to hold and one person to steady. But today I was responsible for two.

Sitting beside me in the front seat, Nellie looked small and fragile. I wasn't sure her tiny arm could be trusted to bear the weight of her oversized purse. The nurse inside of me became a little uncomfortable long before we reached the sign that read, "Welcome to Grand Bay—Watermelon Capital of the World."

Less than twenty-five minutes from the city, in south Mobile County, Grand Bay remains a town more comfortable with the past than the present. Residents, many born and reared there, enjoy a slower lifestyle without superstores, hotels, and chain restaurants. I knew from reading *The Mobile Register* that a new place had opened in Grand Bay, Miss Ann's Kitchen. The article reported that Ann served lunches, made cakes, and catered at her place just beyond the post office on Highway 90.

The sisters still remembered the streets in the town they called home. I followed their directions, and by midmorning we were in the restaurant's parking lot. I wanted to make certain Ann was up this morning and cooking.

Leaving the air-conditioned car running, I cautiously crossed the gravel-covered parking lot and climbed the steps of the small yellow frame structure. An aroma that could only be homemade dressing clung to the hot, heavy air. *Thank You, Lord*, I silently prayed. *They need to eat, and You knew I couldn't take these ladies to the local truck stop!*

The front door required a strong, quick shove before it opened. I stepped inside, and I did not like what I saw. One sweeping view of the tiny space and I knew. Ann prepared home-cooked *take-out* lunches.

Ann listened intently as I explained my dilemma. She reached for her telephone and began dialing before she responded to me. "Savannah's, the florist shop up the street, has a break room where the employees eat. Don't you worry; they won't mind. . . . Hello, Sandy? Ann. Lady from Mobile has her daddy's two elderly relatives here for the day. They need a place to eat. Can you fix up the break room? They might not be able to sit on those stools at the tall table. Maybe you should set up something else in there for them."

Ann hung up the telephone and turned back to me. "All taken care of. White meat or dark on those plates? It'll be ready about twelve."

I explained to Rosalie and Nellie we would have a wonderful lunch at noon, and we would be eating in the floral shop up the street.

"Eating at the florist?" Nellie questioned.

"Yes, we will pick up our lunch here and then be special guests today at Savannah's."

They were understandably confused about the location but happy to be special guests.

I followed their directions to Gaston Loop Road, and Nellie pointed out where the old home place once stood. "This land was homesteaded by our grandfather," Nellie said.

"And he was your great-grandfather," Rosalie added. The two sisters identified homes of other relatives. They attempted to place each relative on the appropriate limb of our family tree. We rambled through the rich farmland while they reminisced.

"We wore homemade feed sack dresses to school. Mama tried to get two feed sacks that matched. It took two sacks to make one dress," Rosalie recalled. "Papa planted almost everything we ate. And I can still smell that sugarcane juice cooking when we made molasses at Uncle Ellis's cane mill on chilly fall mornings."

The parking lot was nearly filled when we returned to pick up lunch. I squeezed my Toyota into the last shady space. "Taking dessert orders," I said after I described the pies and cakes I had seen earlier.

In unison they replied, "Let's go in and see what looks best!"

I recalled the uneven gravel surface of the parking lot. I mentally groaned as I verbally cautioned them to be very careful. Only when we were all three safe on the porch was I able to relax—albeit momentarily.

Before I realized what was happening, Nellie stumbled and tumbled headfirst into the waiting area. It was so filled with customers, there was hardly anywhere for her to land. She managed to find enough room for her head to hit the floor. I immediately saw blood.

Reacting as quickly as the trained personnel in an emergency room, Ann and her customers grabbed clean paper napkins and applied pressure while reassuring Nellie. Everyone wanted to do something. A concerned young man dressed in khakis offered to call 911. We chose to wait a few minutes to see if the bleeding stopped. Hospitality, reaching out to others in love, was portrayed beautifully on that hot August morning.

Nellie, more embarrassed than injured, quickly recovered and insisted on getting up. While covering her wound, no longer bleeding, with a fresh napkin, she chose her dessert. "I am ready to go to our special place to eat," she declared to everyone.

At Savannah's Flowers and Fine Gifts we found more small-town Southern hospitality: a sweet fragrance, a warm greeting, and cool refreshing air. "You must be the people from Mobile," Sandy said as I introduced the group and she led us to the break room. The tall table and four stools had been pushed into a corner and replaced with a card table covered with white linen and red roses. Rosalie and Nellie knew they were special guests.

We ate and talked and laughed. Framed reprints of faded turn-of-the-century pictures provided a gallery where the sisters identified youthful likenesses of family members. "That's Uncle Martin's girls, Lora and Dora," they exclaimed as they viewed the photo of two young girls eating a huge slice of watermelon. Rosalie found a picture of her high school best friend, Margaret Pierson.

"She rides in the Christmas parade every year," Sandy said. She invited us to return in December for the parade and "Christmas in the Country."

Rosalie changed the focus of our conversation back to Mobile and a historic downtown hotel. "In its day the Battle House was the place in Mobile to go—the place to be seen. We used to think when we went to the Battle House we had been *somewhere*. But today we have *really* been somewhere! It's been a grand day."

I smiled and nodded absentmindedly. My intent had been to provide hospitality to distant cousins dear to me. Instead I was a mere spectator watching as the day unfolded. The people of Grand Bay had provided hospitality. They had opened their doors and their hearts in love to total strangers.

You, too, may want to plan a short outing for someone you love. The investment you make of time, money, and effort is minimal. But the return on your investment is great—both to the recipient of your hospitality and to you, as you reach out in love.

PRACTICAL POINTERS

Use this list to trigger your own ideas—and invite someone you know on an outing of love.

- a Memorial Day parade
- a town fair
- Christmas shopping
- a drive in the country to look at fall foliage
- a concert in the park
- a picnic to a nearby nature preserve
- an art museum

GLIMPSES
*There is an emanation
from the heart in genuine hospitality
which cannot be described
but is immediately felt,
and puts the stranger at once at his ease.*

WASHINGTON IRVING

Neighborhood Hospitality

Thy word is a lamp unto my feet,
and a light unto my path.

PSALM 119:105 KJV

On Tuesday, December 14, 1999, the temperature was chilly in Mobile, Alabama. Don and I stepped outside the front door of our home into the semidarkness of a picturesque wonderland. I set the tray of warm chocolate chip cookies on a small table beside the door and stood still to savor the moment. And I thought, *There is only one element that could have made this scene more beautiful—and the likelihood of snow in Mobile is minimal to zero.*

Illuminaries lined the sidewalks of our four-street seventy-home subdivision. Lighted votive candles, securely embedded in paper bags filled with sand,

and the lights of Christmas both inside and outside homes all joined hands to provide an almost mystical scene. Christmas music filtered through the darkness, becoming a blend of traditional carols and solo saxophone. Tonight Bienville Woods subdivision experienced its first Mobile by Candlelight.

The air was full of excitement, even revelry, as adults and children alike opened doors, ventured to the sidewalks, and then into the streets. Surely no one, even those who planned and organized the effort, anticipated the magic of the evening.

Mobile by Candlelight is a city-sponsored event that precedes our downtown New Year's Eve celebration, First Night Mobile. In contrast to the larger gathering, Mobile by Candlelight provides a more intimate arena for neighbors to meet, visit, and provide hospitality to one another.

My next-door neighbor, Paulette, our subdivision chairman, called after Thanksgiving to ask if I would serve on the committee. It happened to be the day after I refused to serve on a committee at church; I had made bold statements to Don about what I would and would not do, insisting I was "taking control of my life again." . . . So I told Paulette I would be happy to be part of this interesting idea. And Don gave me that "I knew you didn't mean what you said" look.

The first meeting was more than a little embarrassing. After living in the subdivision six years, I met some of my neighbors for the first time. But as I listened to others introduce themselves, I realized I wasn't the only one who did not know all the neighbors. The planning meeting became a hospitality tool as Paulette served light refreshments and long-term neighbors chatted, some for the first time.

Our task was simple. Volunteers would contact families on their assigned street. Copies of a fact sheet including date and time and how to make illuminaries would be left with each resident. Outside snacks were mentioned but stressed as optional. I volunteered for my street, only to realize that I had never met two more families on the street!

Our group met for one follow-up meeting. Street captains reported favorable responses from the families they had contacted. Two short meetings, a minimal effort on the part of a small group of women, and now we were experiencing a night to remember!

The weather was not the only thing that cooperated that night. With almost a hundred percent participation, Bienville Woods was the place to be for neighborhood hospitality at its finest. With most porch lights turned off or dimmed for the night, the candle-light produced a magical glow.

But the most beautiful sight to me was the people. Families pushed strollers filled with babies and led older toddlers along by hand. Husbands and wives stood in the middle of our streets meeting neighbors for the first time. Groups gathered on front porches to enjoy sausage biscuits, while the family who baked the biscuits enjoyed cider from a Crock-Pot with friends on another street.

Even though the weather was nippy, older couples stood in open doorways or on porches to watch the activity and enjoy warm chocolate chip cookies brought to their door by friends. I stood in the middle of my street and listened to the excitement. *This,* I thought, *is neighborhood hospitality at its finest. There is hope as we move into a new millennium!*

PRACTICAL POINTERS

Become a trendsetter in your neighborhood. For more information on how to begin your own neighborhood or citywide candlelight celebration, contact:

Andrea Wilson or Herb Scott
Office of Special Events
2900 Dauphin Street
Mobile, Alabama 36606
E-mail: hscott@ci.mobile.al.us

GLIMPSES
*A single beam of light can change
the face of a landscape. . .
like the entrance of Christ
into the heart.*

BONNIE RICKNER JENSEN

Impromptu Hospitality

I thank my God upon every remembrance of you.

PHILIPPIANS 1:3 KJV

On a Friday morning in August 1998, I was complacently thinking that everything was ready for our Sunday school party scheduled for that evening. And then I opened the newspaper and read that a major hurricane, Georges, was swirling in the Gulf of Mexico toward Mobile, Alabama.

Hurriedly, we stocked nonperishable food, filled plastic containers with fresh water, and stored the outside furniture and flowers. The television remained tuned to the Weather Channel while Don considered canceling the party.

Later reports of the forward movement of the storm indicated that it would not likely make landfall until Sunday. The party was held as scheduled. Our children made periodic phone calls urging us to leave home and travel north. We took a "wait and see" approach. But while we waited, I made chicken salad, a big pot of gumbo, and cooked an assortment of other dishes. Hurricane preparation always includes food that can be warmed by (and shared with) someone who owns a gas stove.

PRACTICAL POINTERS

Try this gumbo recipe for your own impromptu hospitality. Make it a day or two ahead of time and keep it on hand; it only improves with time.

½ cup chopped celery   ½ cup chopped
½ cup chopped onions   green pepper

Combine in a small bowl and reserve. Then combine the following four ingredients in a plastic or paper bag:

2 tsp ground red pepper   1 tsp black pepper
1 ½ tsp salt   1 tsp garlic powder

Add to bag and shake until completely covered: 1 whole chicken (about 3 lbs) cut into pieces. Add and shake again: ½ cup flour.

Heat in a large cast iron skillet over medium heat: 2–4 tbsp vegetable oil. Add the chicken and brown on all sides for 5–10 minutes. Remove and set aside. Then add to skillet:

½ cup vegetable oil   ½ cup flour

Cook, stirring often, over medium-low heat until the mixture turns reddish brown. (This is called "roux.") Don't allow the roux to burn. Remove from heat, add the vegetables, and stir until the roux stops bubbling. Add the roux and vegetables to a soup pot with 8 cups chicken stock. Bring to a boil, whisking constantly. Reduce heat and add chicken; simmer until chicken is cooked through (about 30–45 min.). Remove the chicken from the pot and take out the skin and bones; shred the meat and reserve. Stir into the soup pot:

12 oz sausage, cut into thin slices or small cubes
1 tbsp chopped garlic

Simmer until the sausage is cooked through

(about 10 min.). Stir in the chicken meat with

½ cup chopped scallions	salt to taste
hot sauce to taste	

All Sunday church services were cancelled, but Sunday morning the storm was still hours away. The weather reports indicated Mobile would not get a direct hit, and we made the decision to remain in town. Suddenly, we realized we were at home with a refrigerator filled with food and nothing to do except wait. We invited the next-door neighbors for lunch.

The hodgepodge meal was wonderful; the afternoon fellowship was great (even though we listened intently to each weather update). If we had consulted calendars, we could not have planned a six-hour time span to be with busy neighbors. The threatening storm gave us an opportunity to spend time with these friends—a rare treat that we seized. The storm arrived late Sunday night without the gusto originally anticipated.

In years past, before everyone closed doors and turned on the air conditioners, impromptu hospitality was the norm. As a young couple with one child, we were recipients of one such invitation on a Sunday night in 1961. We were new in the city and in our church. As we left the auditorium after the evening worship service, Mayme turned toward us and said, "Come on to the house. We live just down the highway. We'll make some coffee and find something to eat."

I don't recall what we ate or many specifics about the night, but that was an important night. These acquaintances had not prepared for us to come, nor did they plan ahead to invite us. They simply issued an invitation from their hearts of love.

I recently shared that story with Mayme and her husband, Clent. Neither remembers the particular occasion. Impromptu hospitality was their lifestyle. It still is today.

Mayme and Clent are musicians. After Christmas last year, I telephoned to ask if we might bring our children to their home for a night of music. Without a moment of hesitation, Mayme said, "Sure, come on over." She sliced cake and made a pot of coffee. They tuned their musical instruments, and we helped ourselves to the snacks.

For more than an hour we enjoyed instrumental

and vocal renditions, closing with "Amazing Grace." Alan and his family were treated to the same down-home Southern hospitality that we had enjoyed when he was just two years old that first Sunday night after church.

One Christmas season Paula intended to have a neighborhood get-together. She woke up late two days before Christmas, telephoned her husband at his office, and said, "Bill, we are having a party tonight." The plan was simple. The house was already decorated, so Paula called and invited neighbors. Those who could not be reached by telephone were not dropped from the guest list. Rather, she drove from house to house, honked her horn to get each neighbor's attention, and offered a "personal invitation." Her home was filled with more than fifty friends celebrating the season.

Birthday celebrations are also important. Sometimes we go out for a special dinner with friends, but Don's 1999 birthday fell on a Wednesday, a night we attend church. The once-a-year homemade German chocolate cake was much too grand to be eaten alone. I called several couples and invited them to come after church for cake and coffee. Everyone came! A spontaneous telephone call met with more success than other times when formal invitations were mailed. On Thursday and Friday nights other couples enjoyed the still-delicious birthday cake—all invited impromptu!

Well known in her community for her hospitality, Midge received an unexpected early morning telephone call. A friend was in town and wanted to come by for a quick visit. Her home was known to be a gathering place for friends.

But as she surveyed her immediate surroundings, she realized that today her home was also a gathering place for dust. Sunshine filtering through a window revealed a thick covering of dust on the television screen. There was no time to clean or even straighten. With her finger Midge wrote "HI" in large bold letters across the television screen—then welcomed her guests who were knocking on her front door.

Chester and Pat invited two couples for a special omelet and hash brown potato breakfast one Saturday morning. A van outing followed with a late lunch in a nearby town. By midafternoon the group headed home, browsing in antique shops along the way. Afterward, the three couples stood in Chester's front yard, still visiting, as darkness approached. He invited everyone in for coffee, and finally, at nine P.M., twelve full hours after arrival time, the visitors left. It has been almost ten years since then, and the group keeps asking for the date of the next omelet breakfast. His standard reply: "I am afraid if I invite you for breakfast, you'll stay for afternoon coffee, and I am never sure when I will have twelve hours to spare!"

There is a mystical characteristic that surrounds impromptu gatherings. Could it be that an unexpected special treat is more exciting than a planned activity? Perhaps the surprise turns a humdrum day into something exciting. Or does the magic happen simply because someone reached out from a heart of love and called to ask, "Can you come to our home today?"

GLIMPSES

You have been good to me.
Somehow I feel as if it was
what Jesus would do.

CHARLES SHELDON,
In His Steps

Planning a Big Celebration

"A certain man was preparing a great banquet
and invited many guests. . . .
Then the master told his servant,
'Go out to the roads and country lanes
and make them come in,
so that my house will be full.'"

LUKE 14:16, 23 NIV

Nearly forty years have passed since Don sliced his gravy and the first preachers came to eat. We bought and built houses, reared children, planned weddings, and birthed grandchildren. And we continued to celebrate at home.

One warm August morning, Don and I left our

upstate New York hotel to ramble for a day in the hills of Vermont. I had picked up brochures in the hotel lobby, and I thought this would be a good day to discuss plans for the special anniversary we would celebrate in December.

As we wound through villages of yesteryear, I directed the conversation to December and the wedding anniversary. My suggestions came quickly: New York hotels, Broadway plays, and world-famous dining experiences. Don replied, "New York City sounds like a great idea. . . ." His words were followed by a long silence. "Or we could celebrate at home with our friends."

I continued to read aloud *The Best of Broadway*. In response he mused, "We haven't had a large group at this house, have we?" I didn't answer. He already knew the answer to that question, and I knew where this conversation was heading. "Barbara (not the usual "Honey," but "Barbara"), we will only celebrate our fortieth anniversary once. Let's celebrate at home surrounded by people we love."

We don't often have a big party—rather one small event follows another providing a perpetual celebration. However, the time had come for us to have a *big* celebration.

So I reached into my travel office (backseat of the

rental car) for my calendar. We decided on the December date. We knew some would come early and others would find a later hour more convenient, so we chose a four-hour time span. We hoped that some would come and stay. (Many did, and we loved it!)

Meanwhile, as we made our plans, we passed beautiful white churches in quaint Vermont villages. The place for our celebration was already chosen. If we weren't going to New York City, we would celebrate in our home. I was already getting excited about opening our home to a large group of friends.

Don took a "friend naming jaunt" down memory lane, reciting names from bygone years. I dug out the church directory from a stack of folders, and we made a list of people, many whose friendship spanned decades. We wanted to invite *everyone*, but we knew we should limit the guest list to a manageable number. We didn't want to create a night of chaos!

After ordering brunch on the sunporch of a picturesque Vermont inn, my mind continued to party. Considering this was a milestone anniversary, we talked about a formal theme with roses, chamber music, and fancy party food. Decorating one's own home is easy, especially if the gathering is during the Christmas season. We were almost through decorating with candlelight inside and luminaries outside as we pulled into the parking lot of the Vonn Trapp Family Inn.

How exciting to plan a big celebration! And what a lovely place for a Sunday afternoon hike.

By late afternoon we had recovered sufficiently from brunch to devour delicious Ben and Jerry's homemade ice cream. And as we ate, our minds quite naturally turned to food—for the December celebration that we were enjoying in August. The menu was complete—crab mornay, snappy cheese wafers, ham and poppy-seed mini croissant sandwiches, cheese, and fruit. We sighed with satisfaction as we savored the last moment of the Vermont Sunday evening. We would have an anniversary cake and punch served from a cut-glass bowl graced with floating candles. We used the "cater" word, albeit very briefly, because I decided I wanted to prepare the food—with love.

Invitations would have a pretty holiday look and a message that made no mention of our wedding anniversary. Our intent was to focus on honoring friends and family who had contributed to our forty years of happiness.

Entertainment might be a problem, we thought, as musicians have busy schedules during the holiday season. We brainstormed to come up with possibilities—friends, students. But at this late hour, creative thinking was starting to tax our tired brains.

I spent the last few miles of the return trip in deep thought. We hit an obstacle—not one in the road, but a party obstacle as I began to have doubts. At least one moment of panic always rears its ugly head when we plan to open the doors of our home. How could I serve so many people and still enjoy myself? I envisioned *missing* the party as I replenished sandwich trays. I blurted, "Don, I can't do it!"

"You can't do what?" He was through planning parties and was planning his work schedule for the next day.

"I can't do everything and still enjoy the party," I moaned.

"So get some help, someone who doesn't know our friends." Simple problem, simple solution: Don's standard for solving any problem.

We chatted again about opening our home, and once more my excitement grew. Before we pulled into the parking lot of our hotel, we had thoroughly planned every aspect of the December celebration. It would be hard to wait four months.

PRACTICAL POINTERS

Planning for a big (or small) celebration? Follow these ten easy steps:

- Make a decision to have a party.
- Put the time and the date on your calendar—in ink.
- Compile the guest list.
- Decide on a location.
- Choose a theme.
- Consider decorations.
- Make or buy invitations.
- Plan a menu.
- Ask for help!
- Plan to have a wonderful time.

GLIMPSES

*Joy is a net of love by which
we can capture souls. . . .
God loves the person who gives with joy.
Whoever gives with joy gives more.*
MOTHER TERESA, *The Love of Christ*

It's a Piece of Cake

Therefore let us keep the feast.
1 CORINTHIANS 5:8 KJV

Something unusual happened in Mobile on December 18, 1996. A heavy snow (for the Deep South) fell the day before our long-anticipated anniversary celebration. This was the special evening we had planned while touring Vermont, but in our wildest dreams we would never have thought to include snow in this Southern scene!

As our guests arrived, one couple paused on the front sidewalk to enjoy the cold crisp night air and patchy remnants of snow. Surrounded by soft lighting and chamber music filtering from inside, the wife said, "Stand still. We are experiencing a moment in time."

Other guests remembered at least one more moment that night. Candles floating in the punch melted the plastic dipper, rendering it useless. A friend who was helping me whispered, "Do you have another punch ladle?" I spotted my next-door neighbor, whispered in her ear, and she darted out the door. She returned momentarily with a replacement dipper to rescue thirsty guests. Not to worry!

"And what," you might ask, "would you have done if your neighbor had not been present or did not own a ladle?" Plan B would have gone into effect—the stainless steel soup ladle, a punch cup, or a paper cup. I hope I never allow a piece of melted plastic to spoil my evening.

Perfect gatherings occur rarely. Perhaps they come more often at your house, but almost never at mine. Something unexpected usually happens. Rolls refuse to rise, a thunderstorm erupts as the first guests arrive, or the telephone rings while someone blesses the food. The answer? Never plan to have a perfect evening; rather, plan to have a great evening. Refuse to allow flat rolls, Ma Bell, or even a thunderstorm to rain on your hospitality parade.

Some live with Murphy's Hospitality Law permanently attached to their guest list. They are certain whatever can happen will happen and just may be worse than they can even imagine. Fearing something will go wrong, these people rarely invite others to their home.

True, sometimes things do not work out as well as

we would like. But the sun always rises the next morning. Hospitality means we enjoy each other—not perfection.

A friend remembers entertaining fifty people for a buffet dinner in Honduras. Suddenly, the electricity went off, ending the recorded music and dancing. However, candles were found to provide enough light for a memorable evening.

On another occasion her husband invited twelve people for dinner on the Saturday before Easter. Being fairly new in Honduras, the family didn't realize that almost everything closed down the week before Easter. She related, "I didn't really get upset. I was used to entertaining. The main dish was no trouble because we had a freezer with lots of meat and lobster. And the vegetables could always be bought fresh in the open market. But what could I do about dessert? Not a single bakery was open all week. I looked in my pantry and found one can of cherry pie filling and one can of apple pie filling we had brought in our shipment from the United States. But if I made two separate pies and ten people wanted cherry and no one wanted apple, what would I do? So I mixed them together, put in some cinnamon and nutmeg, a little almond extract, and a few blanched almonds. I put the whole thing in a 9-by-12 baking dish and dotted butter on top. Then I mixed up sweet pie dough, sprinkled it over the top, and baked the dish until it bubbled and the crust was lightly browned. I whipped some cream and served the pie in little bowls with toasted almonds over the top. Everybody raved over the dish, so I quit worrying." (The recipe was used later when her church compiled a cookbook.)

No need to worry. Hospitality is a piece of cake —or sometimes pie!

This same friend relates details of another not-so-perfect evening. "There was the time in Venezuela when my guests were sitting in the living room after dinner having coffee—and a four-foot snake slithered across the marble floor. Pandemonium!" And the sun did rise the next morning!

Another friend planned an outside crawfish boil. When she left the pot unattended, the critters, fighting to escape the hot water, pushed the lid off the boiler. She returned in time to retrieve the fleeing entrées and return them to the cooker.

A pastor husband often invited guests attending the Sunday morning worship service to join his family for lunch. The wife routinely prepared for extras at her table. One Sunday a large roast was left in the oven and visitors accompanied the pastor's family home after church, only to find the oven cold and the roast still partially frozen.

The visitors knew the art of roast preparation in a microwave and soon the entrée and the other dishes were ready.

And Judy. Poor Judy. On April first, she decided to pull a joke on her husband and trash the front yard. A friend helped fill the yard with old tires, flowerpots, boards, lots of hubcaps, and even a junked car. Her husband came home at the regular time but not alone. A prim and proper British lady who had arrived unexpectedly earlier in the day accompanied him. She was the husband's boss.

You will recall that Lady Macbeth once planned a huge dinner party. After the guests arrived and were seated, her husband announced to his wife and the group that he had murdered his best friend. Talk about spoiling a dinner party! Surely nothing that happens at your table will ever compare!

If I scorch the gumbo as guests are entering the front door, I will add enough Cajun seasoning to disguise the burnt taste. (My friend did.) If I lose an acrylic nail while I'm mixing enchiladas for company, I will simply summon my husband to the kitchen to unroll and search. (Another friend's adventure.)

Lady Macbeth's party is my standard. In comparison, whatever happens at my house is a piece of cake.

PRACTICAL POINTERS

Try serving "a piece of cake" from this easy recipe for Applesauce Cake:

2 ¼ cups flour
1 tsp salt
1 tsp baking soda
1 tsp cinnamon
½ cup soft butter or margarine

1 cup molasses
1 egg
1 cup applesauce
¾ cup raisins

Combine ingredients and bake in 8-inch square pan for 40–45 minutes at 350 degrees. Sprinkle with confectioner's sugar and serve.

GLIMPSES
*The test of pleasure is
the memory it leaves behind.*
JEAN PAUL RICHTER

Tips for Giving a Party Everyone Will Love

(Even the Hostess!)

Be joyful at your Feast. . . .
DEUTERONOMY 16:14 NIV

The year was 1963. We were living in our tiny brick starter house, and it was time for an extended family bridal shower, a major event in our large family. I volunteered. There was likely some skepticism among the mature, seasoned hostesses, my mother's generation, who had larger homes, silver trays, and fine china. There likely was also a collective sigh of relief from the same group, my mother and her sisters, as they passed the family bridal shower torch to my generation.

I was a novice, yet I was excited. At last the little girl inside of me was going to have a *real* tea party. The guest list came by mail from the bride-to-be, only family but a long list. Standing in the middle of my living room, I mentally calculated how many bodies would fit and quickly decided the term "standing room only" might take on new meaning in our family. Realizing that standing for this occasion was not the best solution, I counted spaces on the long couch, chairs in my house, and then borrowed folding chairs from our church.

Everyone came. The room was packed with people, many of whom were seated on the bare floor. I looked around and saw everyone laughing, passing gifts, and congratulating the bride. And I thought, *They are having a good time.* I realized in that moment that people don't mind being crowded if they are enjoying themselves—so I relaxed and enjoyed my party.

My learning experience did not end with the departure of the last guest. After forty years I am still learning. Each time I invite guests, I recognize the importance of what I have found to be the three most important hospitality words:

- Organize.
- Simplify.

- Relax!

If I invite a couple for dinner or one hundred for open house, the rules remain the same. The preparation is simply tailored to fit the particular occasion.

Organize! The moment the idea is conceived, grab a notebook and pen. When a date and time is chosen, begin a "time line"—a loose outline of everything you will need to do from "Make a guest list" to "Light the candles before the guests arrive," and everything in between. Use your notebook to jot down ideas, plan the menu, and start a grocery list. Keep your planning book with you and pick up items (napkins, favors, or film) as you do regular shopping.

Choose guests who are compatible but not necessarily friends or even acquaintances. When planning for a large group, include new neighbors or others who have not been to your home. When guests are not familiar with one another, name tags are helpful even though the group is small.

Simplify! Make your menu based on preparation time and what your budget will easily allow. Appetizers can be time consuming. Instead, use simple dips and crackers or purchase prepared appetizers at a local wholesale club. Most vegetable casseroles and many desserts can be prepared ahead and frozen. Avoid recipes requiring last-minute preparation. On the day of the event the smart hostess will only need to toss a salad and prepare the entrée.

My favorite part of preparing for a dinner party is the table preparation. Begin early, gathering items for a centerpiece, pulling out dishes to match the occasion, and folding the napkins. "Play house," using first one and then another tablecloth. If you aren't satisfied with the way the table looks, remove the cloth and table pad. Try place mats and use a mirror for the center of the table. Cover this with lamps or candlesticks. Play with your "pretties" until you find a look to match the occasion. Finish the table—centerpiece and candles, china, crystal and silver, even salt and pepper shakers—the day *before* you are expecting guests. A box of matches on the plate of the host or hostess becomes a cue to light the candles before guests are seated. Placing favors near the front door is a reminder to hand them to guests as they leave.

Accept help from friends who offer. Don and I recently hosted a dinner party in honor of a retiree. My desire was to make this an elegant evening of fellowship and dining. After I thoroughly considered the two future speaking engagements that required preparation, a house that needed cleaning, and an editor expecting a manuscript, I accepted the offer of help from the other guests. One prepared a salad and another a dessert, allowing time for me to prepare special appetizers.

Relax! On the day of your event the time line for preparation ends three hours prior to the time guests are expected. If your dinner is scheduled for seven, your preparations (other than putting the entrée in the oven and tossing the salad) should be completed by four P.M. Take a shower, a nap, and eat a snack. (We usually snack on appetizers.) Now you are ready to dress for the occasion. When your guests arrive, you are rested, ready, and eager to enjoy them.

Of course you can have everything completed by four P.M. If the party hour were at four P.M. you would be ready. Pretend your guests will arrive at four and allow yourself time to relax. You will be glad that you did.

PRACTICAL POINTERS

When serving appetizers or a buffet meal, your guests don't need to eat as soon as they arrive. Don't hurry the evening. Allow a full hour for all guests to assemble, snack, and socialize. Relax and enjoy yourself—the party has begun.

Serve a seated dinner leisurely. If appetizers are followed by a salad, allow fifteen minutes after finishing salads before beginning to serve the main course. Dessert and coffee are enjoyed after guests have had time to fellowship.

Organizing is important. Simplifying decreases stress in the life of a hostess (and her husband). However, the most important discovery of my hospitality career occurred the night I realized that I enjoy myself more if I am rested and relaxed.

And if I enjoy myself, my guests will do the same.

GLIMPSES
There is no greatness where there is not simplicity.

LEO TOLSTOY

It's the Little Things That Count

This is my commandment,
That ye love one another, as I have loved you.

JOHN 15:12 KJV

Don was approaching his fiftieth birthday. It seemed so monumental—having survived and for the most part enjoyed a half century of life. I realized this was a good reason to have a party. Or, perhaps, just a good *excuse*. At our house any excuse is a good excuse to have a party.

To pull off the surprise for Don, I knew I needed to get off to an early start. Busy prospective guests would need to know weeks ahead to reserve the date. I chose a date, mailed a "pre" invitation, and asked for a response from each couple. I sketched a crude image of a finger on the front of a card. A short piece of string inserted through two small openings was tied around the finger with a message printed below: "Don't Forget! Plan to attend a surprise birthday party for Don Sims on August 25, 1983. More information to follow. Regrets only."

The pre-invitation was something different and unusual. The card caught the attention of guests and sparked interest in the upcoming event. And it achieved my goal. Invited guests knew well in advance and put the date on their calendars. Everyone invited attended! (One creative guest wore the string on his finger to the party. There is one in every crowd!)

Invitations add to the excitement as guests look forward to an event. On the selected date, place cards speak personally to each person, saying, "I am glad you came." Favors, too, are a permanent reminder of a special time with friends. Individually these are little things, but collectively they make a difference. Little things do count!

Invitations can be as elaborate as engraved cards for a fiftieth anniversary or as casual as a handwritten note (with a string attached). Creative ideas and your computer can provide everything necessary for unique ways to invite people to "party." Attractive theme invitations are also available in specialty card shops. Many of these stores offer imprinting at a nominal fee.

After a cruise, Don and I hosted a dinner at our house using a nautical theme. For the invitation we used a computer-generated, full-page replica of the cruise line Daily Activity sheet, adorned with the cruise line emblem. Information, such as time, place, attire, and activities for the evening, was listed. We hand-delivered the invitations to each home, just as the Daily Activity sheets had been personally delivered to cabins on the ship.

Ideas for place cards are endless when one considers a theme lunch or dinner. For a casual summer luncheon, slice a lemon or lime through the skin to the middle of the fruit. Write the guest's name at the top of a card, and slide the card inside the "fruit place card holder." Place on a coaster or a few fresh leaves at each place setting.

A miniature bottle of Tabasco with a name tag attached makes a unique place card for a Cajun cooking dinner and also serves as a take-home favor. Chili seasoning packages in brown bags with names printed on the bags serve as both place cards and favors for a Western party. Or consider a small cactus planted in a clay pot. Use florist picks to display the names of the guests.

Miniature picture frames double as place cards and favors. Print names on plain or decorative paper and insert in a small inexpensive frame for each person (or couple). Take snapshots during the evening and have them developed for guests. They can place the photos in their frames later as a reminder of a special time together.

PRACTICAL POINTERS

The list of inexpensive favors is endless:

- bookmarks
- chocolates
- dainty handkerchiefs
- small inspirational books
- special blends of tea
- jelly in small glass jars
- homemade cookies in a basket
- beans packaged with a recipe for soup
- A favorite devotional thought or recipe printed from the computer on pretty paper is

economical when your guest list is lengthy. Roll papers and secure with a rubber band, then tie with a pretty ribbon and remove the rubber band.

• Place the favors in a basket near the front door and hand to guests as they exit.

Little things do make a difference. Invest in a pretty guest book for visitors to sign. Choose appropriate music for the occasion. Use candles and oil lamps for atmosphere. Begin a hospitality journal, a permanent record of little things. Indicate who drinks regular and who prefers decaf, sweetened or unsweetened tea, and the food allergies of your guests. The journal might also include a prayer list of those who come to visit who are hurting, ill, lonely, or searching for truth.

A beautiful story of love was shared with me recently. One lady has kept a hospitality journal all of her adult life. She continues to make entries today, even though she has passed her ninety-fifth birthday. What a legacy this dear lady has preserved for her family!

Little things mean a lot. They send a message of love. And love always makes a difference.

GLIMPSES
Every true friend is a glimpse of God.

LUCY LARCOM

Teaching Children to Reach Out to Others

Let your light so shine before men,
that they may see your good works,
and glorify your Father which is in heaven.
MATTHEW 5:16 KJV

Turkey and dressing, pumpkin pies, football and family feasts. . .but not everyone has experienced these all-American Thanksgiving traditions. A youth leader decided that his youth choir needed to reach out to a family less fortunate than themselves at Thanksgiving time. They chose a single mother with three small children to be the recipient of a Thanksgiving blessing from the choir.

The mother, a custodian at a nearby college, was living in substandard housing, but her requests were simple—groceries and warm blankets. The adults involved in this project felt strongly that the young people should do more than give money for these items. Like many of today's youth, they only crossed paths with other families like themselves, never seeing many individuals with genuine need. So members of the youth choir, their leader, and his six-year-old son delivered grocery gift certificates and blankets to the mother's work site. She was so overwhelmed with the kindness shown to her by the group that she asked for permission to hug them. The six-year-old stepped forward quickly and said, "I'm a great hugger!"

Later he asked his father, "Why did the lady ask if it was okay to hug us?" This was the first time he had realized that some people did not live like he did, people who had few material possessions, people who were not even sure they were worthy of a hug.

Nowhere in our society is the "I, Me, and Mine" concept more prevalent than in the lives of our children. Parents, teachers, and churches are challenged to define hospitality in childlike terms. Children learn best by example. Those children who have the opportunity to reach out to others as children are more likely to participate in hands-on activities when they are adults. While saving money for foreign missionaries and world hunger is beneficial for children, their lives can be changed forever when they deliver a Christmas tree to a needy family and stay to help the family decorate the tree.

Almost twenty years earlier, the father of the six-year-old hugger had learned firsthand about poverty. He was fifteen and accompanied *his* father to deliver Christmas packages and food items to a needy family who was not expecting to have a Christmas celebration. They did not even dream of having a tree to decorate.

The family's home was in a crime-ridden impoverished area of the city. The father worked for minimum wage to support the family of six. The mother had a serious neurological disease that had been passed to one son. Medical expenses, food for the family, rent, and gasoline for the family car left no money for a Christmas celebration.

The family was "adopted." Christmas was not only delivered, it was also experienced. The host family purchased food necessary for preparing a traditional Christmas dinner and stuffed a stocking with a gift certificate for a turkey the family would pick up just prior to Christmas. A Sunday school class bought appropriate gifts for each family member, and the host family purchased additional special gift items. A date and time were set for the father and fifteen-year-old son to make the delivery.

The son knew the home would be different. It might be tidy, but it would likely smell of stale cigarette smoke. Upholstered furniture would be soiled and ragged. "Should we leave the gifts in the boxes or put them under the Christmas tree?" he asked—and learned the family would not have a tree. "But we have an artificial tree in the attic," he said, "and old ornaments we don't use anymore. And colored strings of lights we used before we bought the new ones. We can make a tree for them!"

And he did make a tree—with the help of the four children as their parents watched in awe. The sparkle in the eyes of the tree trimmers that night likely outshone the lights on the tree.

It is not surprising that the now grown-up fifteen-year-old is the father who took his youth group and young child to deliver joy to another family in another city. Children learn by example to reach out to others.

Another family took their young daughter to a shelter in their city to serve Thanksgiving dinner to the homeless. Once a month she also accompanied her father as he delivered groceries to the city's most desperate citizens. When the daughter was fourteen years old, she volunteered to go to another state to help build a house for a family living in a substandard mobile home.

One mother played the piano at a local nursing home each week for the pleasure of the people who lived there. Her two beautiful young daughters accompanied her and made friends with the residents. The music and interaction with the young girls brought smiles to faces and joy to hearts. But something else important was happening. The mother was teaching her daughters to reach out in love to others two generations beyond themselves.

I called today to check on our youngest granddaughter. Sarah celebrated her first birthday just a few days before Christmas. In the past five days she has made two unplanned visits to her doctor, in addition to two emergency rooms visits in two cities. Our son, Mark, reported that she is fine and he is preparing dinner for company. After all, the night was already planned, and guests were invited weeks ago. I expressed surprise that the party was on, considering everything that happened during the week. His reply? "I knew they wanted to come while the house was decorated for Christmas. Are you not the same mother who taught me, by example, that one does not wait until the children are grown and the house is clean to invite guests for dinner?"

PRACTICAL POINTERS

Activities to teach your children to reach out to others:

- Visit nursing homes. Just the sight of a child's face brightens a senior citizen's day— and helps the child understand the power of a smile.
- Volunteer as a family to pack food baskets for the Salvation Army at Christmastime.
- Encourage your children to draw pictures and make cards to send to shut-ins in your community or church.
- "Adopt" a child in another country through World Vision or another child-support organization, and encourage your children to exchange letters and send small gifts.

(Contact World Vision at P.O. Box 78481, Tacoma, WA 98481-8481.)

- Visit local shelters as a family and ask for particular needs. Encourage your children to sort through their own belongings to donate to those in need.
- *Practice what you preach!*

GLIMPSES

Just as transparent substances,
when subjected to the light,
themselves glitter and give off light,
so does the soul,
illumined by the Holy Spirit,
give light to others. . . .

ST. BASIL

Adopted Grandparents

And whosoever shall give to drink. . .
of cold water only in the name of a disciple,
verily I say unto you,
he shall in no wise lose his reward.

MATTHEW 10:42 KJV

It had been a difficult decision to make. We were departing from a church where we had served for many years. We were leaving more than just the place where we worshiped—we were leaving close friends, special relationships, and memories. But the decision was made. On that May Sunday morning, we joined Lafitte Baptist Church.

The warmth with which we were greeted and welcomed into the church family was comforting. An elderly lady with red hair lingered afterward and walked to the parking lot with us.

She introduced herself as Mary Cunningham. We had mutual friends, so we knew Mrs. Cunningham by reputation. She was a widow, a retired school principal, and for many years she had been a staunch and faithful member in this church fellowship. She spoke to each of us individually, but it was Mark, our twelve-year-old son, with whom she connected immediately. The principal inside her appeared as she asked what grade he was in, where he went to school, and what subject was his favorite.

Months later, we invited Mrs. Cunningham to have Sunday lunch with us. The conversation was so interesting that Mark never left the table. Rather, he sat and listened intently throughout the afternoon. He was enchanted by the stories she told about children she had taught and the faraway places she had visited. We learned that her only child, a son, lived in a distant city.

The afternoon was interrupted by a telephone call telling us that Don's aunt had died. Mrs. Cunningham left immediately but returned later with freshly baked muffins for us to enjoy as we traveled by car to the funeral. On that Sunday afternoon our family discovered a grandmother who lacked a family nearby to grandparent.

Even though Mark had a doting grandmother whom he adored, Mrs. Cunningham added another dimension to his life. She challenged him to achieve his highest potential academically. She told him stories about the great masterpieces of art she had seen and described in detail places he had only read about in books.

While some friends tired of her endless stories, Mark cherished every word and dreamed of someday visiting the places she described. She became his confidant, his buddy, another advocate, another grandmother.

Mrs. Cunningham and my mother also developed a close friendship. They traveled together, and she became a part of our extended family holiday celebrations. Actually she became part of our family. Without realizing what was happening, we adopted a grandparent, and she adopted a family.

The hospitality offered that Sunday afternoon was lasting. Our family reached out in love. A single gesture—an invitation to Sunday lunch—resulted in a fifteen-year friendship bridging three generations.

In years past, grandparents and grandchildren lived in geographical proximity, many times even in the same home. Life was shared daily by three generations. The wisdom of grandparents was passed to grandchildren as stories were told and flowers were planted. Godly grandparents taught Christian virtues. They told Bible stories and lived a Christlike example before their grandchildren.

In today's mobile society, generations are often

physically separated. Hugs come in the form of long-distance telephone calls, and cookies for grandchildren arrive through the U.S. mail in a package, rather than warm and freshly baked. Yet for each grandparent without a resident grandchild to read to, there is also a grandchild who does not have a local grandparent to provide fresh baked cookies and a daily hug.

Some grandparenting relationships just happen. Others are more structured. When Don and I first entered the age to grandparent, we were more formerly adopted into a unique situation. Beverly, a close friend who was single at the time, had adopted a child from India. She asked us to serve as the second set of grandparents. (Before that time I had never thought about children with single parents having only one set of grandparents.) We made a commitment to fulfill that role. Beverly subsequently married, and later she and her husband adopted a second child from India. Twelve years later our lives are richer indeed to have been adopted into this family as surrogate grandparents.

Not all children in homes of single parents arrive from another country on planes. Many are born to single moms. Through death, divorce, or desertion, many other homes have only one parent. This provides a unique opportunity for mature friends to reach out in love. Parents whose married children live in distant cities can choose to show their love in simple ways to a child who needs a local grandparent.

PRACTICAL POINTERS

How can you become an adopted grandparent?

- Take a child to a neighborhood park for a leisurely afternoon.
- Become a support system to the parent.
- Mail cards to the children on holidays and birthdays.
- Invite the family to go to church with you.

There is no greater legacy than to touch the life of a child.

If your own children are young and you are displaced from your family, adopt grandparents for your children. Wisdom and love (and cookies) are available to you. Reach out in love to someone in your neighborhood, church, or workplace who is living far from their extended family. Adopt a Mrs.

Cunningham, a grandparent for your children.

Mrs. Cunningham provided hospitality for our family for many years. She prepared delicious dinners, provided Mark with a bed close to home when we were out of town, and provided lots of love and hugs.

Her last years in Mobile were difficult as she struggled to remain independent. We tried to make life easier for her, to provide the same love she had shared with us over the years. It was then our turn to reach back to her in love.

Was she an *adopted* grandparent? Maybe not. After all, we were blood related—through our Savior.

GLIMPSES
*The greatest gift
we can give one another is
rapt attention to one another's existence.*
SUE ATCHLEY EBAUGH

Joyful Celebrations at Home
(Hay on the Porch and Roses in the Bathtub)

A joyful heart is good medicine. . . .
PROVERBS 17:22 NASB

The invitation card with an Old West motif read:

Please meet us at the hotel where we live.
Saturday, May 18, 1996
Breakfast 9:00–11:00 A.M.
4913 Brooke Court
Don and Barbara Sims
Dress: Casual—Western—Denim

Saturday morning arrived with a bright and

shiny face and deep blue skies. Friends came in a festive mood. The guys sported denim, cowboy hats and boots, and western belts (some with holsters attached). Wives modeled denim jeans, denim jumpers, plaid shirts, and Western jewelry.

Signs made from poster board attached to one-by-one-inch sticks lined the concrete walk to the front door of our home. Each sign described an appropriate behavior for the day.

SHERIFF ON DUTY—PARK HORSES OUTSIDE.
NO CUSSIN' ALLOWED—THAT INCLUDES PREACHERS.
LEAVE ALL GUNS WITH THE SHERIFF.
CLEAN BOOTS BEFORE ENTERING.
TREAT ALL LADIES WITH RESPECT.

Those still not certain of the address were reassured when they spotted the bale of hay (three dollars from a local feed store) on the front porch. A sign on the door read "EMPTY ROOMS HOTEL." Sheriff Don, wearing an official toy sheriff badge, greeted guests. The sheriff's wife wore a denim dress and matching dime-store Western earrings and necklace.

Waylon Jennings and Willie Nelson wailed from

the CD player, while Merle Haggard waited patiently for his turn to sing train songs. John Wayne on the television screen brought scenes from the Old West into the den of our home. An aroma of breakfast food permeated the entire house.

The formal dining room looked a little less than formal. Guns were lying across the table and a lasso hung from the chandelier. The large leafy ficus tree provided a background of greenery at the end of the camouflage-covered dining table. Brunch food was served in pots, skillets, and pans.

Hungry guests filled tin plates and found empty seats at small tables decorated with lanterns, potted cactus, lassos, and kerchiefs. Cowboys—and some cowgirls—made a second trip to the buffet, which included breakfast casserole, deer sausage, cheesy grits, fruit and cheese, bran muffins, coffee cake, and a bagel bar for those eating healthy.

One innovative cowboy dashed into the room and lassoed a female guest before the eyes of the surprised host and hostess. Later a name was randomly (?) drawn from the basket where all cowboys had signed in to choose the "King of the Rodeo." Tony (wisely) picked his wife as queen.

It was a morning of fun and frolic. The cowgirls slipped out to refine their choreographed version of "Happy Trails to You." Before the last good-byes were said, the ladies performed their vocal rendition to the all-male audience.

When the last cowperson left, the sheriff turned to his wife and said, "Honey, that was the best party we have ever had!" I reminded him that he makes that statement after *every* party. His response, "I know, but they get better every time."

While Don and I relish the roles of host and hostess, "Come for dinner" is also a lovely phrase when spoken by a friend. Recipients of the hospitality of friends, Don and I arrived at their front door late one summer afternoon. We stood outside amidst the beauty of a sunset while we breathed in the fragrances of summer flowers. As we stepped through the door, the fragrance became an unmistakable aroma of roses.

Appetizers were served in the den with white grape juice in chilled stemwear. Later, the host escorted guests to the dining table. The hostess had prepared the table with her best china, crystal, and silver. The tablescape was an array of candles and roses. A lovely idea and special touch was an individual crystal vase filled with roses beside each plate. The host and hostess served the gourmet meal in courses.

A separate table, covered with a lace cloth and sprinkled with rose petals, was set up for desserts in another room. The then not-so-hungry guests admired (and somehow devoured) the dessert, "Death by Chocolate." This hostess went more than the second mile. Her guest bathroom tub was half filled with water and rosebuds were floating in the bathtub! A host and hostess who opened their home in love for a celebration of friendship provided a laughter-filled evening of beauty.

PRACTICAL POINTERS

Try your own "Death by Chocolate" using this recipe:

8 oz unsweetened dark
   chocolate, chopped
   into small pieces
$^1/_2$ cup butter
$^2/_3$ cup milk
1 $^1/_4$ cup brown sugar

2 tsp vanilla
2 eggs
$^1/_2$ cup sour cream
2 cups flour
1 tsp baking powder

Melt chocolate with butter and milk, and stir over low heat until smooth. Stir in sugar and vanilla, then combine with other ingredients and pour into 9-inch springform pan. Bake at 350 degrees for 45–55 minutes. Remove from pan and cool. Slice cake in three even layers. Spread each layer with filling and pile on top of each other. Frost top with more filling and dust with confectioner's sugar and cocoa.

FILLING

4 oz dark chocolate, chopped

½ cup butter

2 ¼ cup confectioner's sugar

6 tbsp plain yogurt

Melt chocolate and butter in a saucepan over low heat. Remove from heat and combine with other ingredients.

Sometimes friends need to get together, laugh, and have fun. It is not necessary to have a reason. Perhaps just celebrating friendship is a good enough reason. Any reason is a good reason to get together with friends. We just call it a party.

The world has too long viewed Christians as a somber group. Paul wrote to the church at Corinth, "Always be full of joy in the Lord." And this same Scripture speaks to today's men and women. We have every reason to celebrate, to be joyful. We serve a risen Christ! We need to gather with friends for an evening of fellowship and laughter. Plan a party. Open your heart. Open your home.

GLIMPSES

Give me a positive, practical joy, God.
Help me to live in Your love,
so that Your joy will live in me.

WWJD?

Celebrate the Beginning of a New Year

Greater love hath no man than this,
that a man lay down his life for his friends.
Ye are my friends, if ye do whatsoever I command you.
JOHN 15:13–14 KJV

At midnight a vast array of televised fireworks encircling the earth announcing the arrival of a new century and a New Year, January 1, 2000. It was the world's annual fresh start, a clean page, a new beginning, an opportunity to resolve to eat and drink less, do more, be kinder, and walk more closely with the Savior.

I hate New Year's resolutions. I am sure I began making resolutions as soon as I understood the concept, but I was never able to keep one past New Year's Day. I recall vividly one particular list I had displayed next to my bed; I can visualize the way I printed it, even the way the letters were formed. And I broke each resolution before bedtime.

I was about nine years old when I wrote that list of resolutions on December 31. There were just three entries: "Read my Bible, clean up my room, and feed the rabbit." I never gave them a thought until I climbed into bed New Year's night when I saw the list. I was horrified. I had broken all three resolutions the first day. What to do? I was too sleepy to read my Bible. I definitely wasn't going out in the dark to feed the rabbit. And there was no need to make my bed. I was in it. I felt like I had already failed—and I had 364 more opportunities that year to do the same.

I never recall making a New Year's resolution in my life that I kept all year. They may work for some, but I *really* don't like resolutions. So Don and I came up with a better idea that has worked for us many years. We make goals instead of resolutions. It's almost foolproof. One can hardly "break a goal." Even when we fall short, the goal remains on the horizon within our reach. We just need to work a little longer and harder. We make spiritual, financial, exercise, health, and various other goals. And we make hospitality goals.

One hospitality goal Don made for 2000 is to minister weekly to a senior couple in our city. The couple faithfully attended their local church for many years where they were in charge of the Shut-in Ministry. Now they are unable to attend church and rarely leave home except for doctor appointments. This couple provided hospitality on wheels to others. Now they are the recipients of hospitality, a hot home-cooked meal delivered each Wednesday afternoon to their home.

But the one who delivers the meal does not make it possible for them to stay in their home. That responsibility was assumed by the young couple, Darrell and Vicki, who lives next door. They may not make New Year's resolutions, but they have attained a goal of distinction, reaching out in love by being on call—twenty-four hours every day for next-door neighbors.

Like the bear learning to walk, most Christians want to reach out to others. In the absence of a mother bear to get us motivated, perhaps a hospitality goal each January is one answer. If resolutions work for you, that is good. If they don't, make a goal that is attainable. You can touch many lives in a positive way by aiming toward a goal as simple as "Mail twelve greeting cards to friends next year." Julia A. F. Carney may have received a card or a note from a friend the day she penned these words:

> *Little deeds of kindness,*
> *Little words of love*
> *Help to make earth happy*
> *Like the heavens above.*

PRACTICAL POINTERS

Buy twelve cheery "Thinking of You" cards. Mail one each month to a different shut-in. It will likely be the brightest spot in the day of each recipient. If you miss your goal one month, play catch-up and mail two cards the following month.

Many times we are inspired to do something that would be encouraging to another person. But our thoughts are useless unless acted upon. Make your monthly goal to call someone who is a caregiver. Become an encourager. It will cost you about two hours during the year—a small price to pay for the support it will give to the caregiver.

Those ideas are mere suggestions. Perhaps you already have a burden for a person or a situation. Make a goal. Share your goal with another person. After I share my goals with someone else, I feel more accountable.

Even though I am not where I want to be, as I move along the "Goal Road," I'm not where I used to be either. I am still a student in the school of love, kindness, and reaching out to others. Over and over I fail "Faithfulness 101," but my vision has improved. Almost every day I see an opportunity to take a step I haven't made before, to reach out to someone new. When I miss an opportunity, it is lost forever. But in spite of my failure, I am certain of one fact: On January 1, 2001, I will have a fresh, clean page on which I will write my goals. I also will be given 365 new opportunities to fill the pages with acts of kindness.

And you will be given the same.

GLIMPSES
*When one helps another,
both are strong.*

GERMAN PROVERB

Valentine Celebrations

Let us stop just saying we love each other;
let us really show it by our actions.

1 JOHN 3:18 NLT

February was the month assigned to Raye and Bob to host supper club for a group of longtime friends. Decorations and fun activities focused on Valentine's Day, a season to celebrate romantic love. "Bubba Gump's Shrimp Company," made famous by the movie *Forrest Gump,* provided food for the evening. The fictional company, quite a topic in our area when the movie was released, was located in Bayou La Batre, just a few miles south of Mobile, Alabama.

As the eight couples arrived, their hosts ushered them into festive surroundings. Chandeliers were draped gold and pearl beads. Heart-shaped gold orna-ments retrieved from the Christmas decoration boxes were suspended by fish line and hung at different levels amidst the beads. Dining tables were topped with red and white table covers and sprinkled with tiny red hearts and Hershey's kisses. Candlelight and easy listening romantic music provided the perfect atmosphere.

The evening's menu was actually prepared by the supper club, elevated to new status as members of the "Bubba Gump Shrimp Company" for this occasion. A favorite shrimp offering in our area is gumbo made from a dark roux and served hot and spicy; Raye provided the gumbo and asked five couples to prepare their favorite shrimp dishes. These included shrimp and rice casse-role, boiled shrimp, and shrimp salad. Others brought desserts—rich, dark, decadent chocolate desserts. What would Valentine's Day be without chocolate?

After dinner the men retired to the den, their usual place to chat. But they were greeted with red and white construction paper, heart-shaped doilies, glitter, glue, Magic Markers, and pens. The men were told to make a valentine for their wife. The husband who created the most beautiful and romantic was promised a surprise.

Wives left the room but listened from the

kitchen. Husbands were overheard saying, "I can't believe we are doing this." From the doorway the men could be seen painstakingly working with fingers glued together and glitter flying everywhere. When the valentines were completed, they were displayed side by side on a long table.

Each card was creative and beautiful. Each wife studied the cards carefully. When certain she had discovered the card made by *her* husband, she stood beside him with her choice of the cards. As one might imagine, fun, laughter, and maybe a twinge of nostalgia followed. When much had been said and the last card was chosen, only three wives from the group of eight had correctly identified the cards made by their own husbands!

An award was given to Kathy, one of the wives who chose the correct card. Knowing she was labeled (unjustifiably, of course) as the spender of the group, Kathy had chosen the card with a big dollar sign printed on a white heart-shaped doily. A huge stuffed gorilla with a red heart was ceremoniously awarded to Kathy's husband, Craig, while the other seven "winners" received a giant chocolate kiss wrapped in foil.

Supper clubs within a neighborhood or church allow couples to strengthen friendships through monthly

vship as they celebrate each season. You may have an
opportunity to join a group, or you may choose to form a
new group within your church or neighborhood.

PRACTICAL POINTERS

Perhaps during early February you may want to plan a simple evening with several couples. Serve sugar cookies or cheesecake and steamy mugs of chocolate topped with whipped cream! Include a couple who may be searching for friends to accept and love them.

Let February fourteenth be an opportunity to tell someone in your own special way, "I love you." Write a letter of love to a friend, your mother, or your daughter of any age. Buy a bag of valentines and sign your name on each. Add a short Scripture on love, perhaps, 1 John 3:11: "Love one another." Distribute your cards to residents at a local nursing home. Your own heart will be warmed when you see a spark in the eyes of the recipients as you give of yourself.

The best gift, the best way to reach out in love, is to give a part of ourselves, our time. And sometimes love can be shared in the form of a colorful valentine card! Celebrate this February season of love.

GLIMPSES

Give all you have,
as well as all you are,
a spiritual sacrifice to Him who
withheld not from you His Son,
His only Son. . . .

JOHN WESLEY

Celebrate Spring—
A Time of Blossoms

" 'The winter is past,
the rain is over and gone.
The flowers are springing up and
the time of the singing of birds has come.' "
SONG OF SOLOMON 2:11–12 TLB

Spring may be my favorite season of the year. At this moment I am quite certain it is my favorite season, because our yard, our neighborhood, our entire city is ablaze with color. I want to drink my morning coffee from a flower-covered china cup, repot a plant, sit on my back porch in the swing, and listen to the birds. Or sit outside on the porch in a rocking chair and enjoy an airy piece of music and savor a peaceful cup of tea. I want to unpack the china eggs and bunnies that have been stored too long in dark boxes in the attic.

Yes, today I am *certain*: This is my favorite season, and I want to make every spring day a special occasion. What an unusual privilege awaits us! Christians, much like flowers, have an opportunity to blossom and bring joy to the lives of others.

Celebrate with family. Don and I enjoyed Easter weekend with our son Alan and his family in Knoxville, Tennessee. The Easter Sunday morning service at West Hill Baptist Church was a beautiful musical celebration of the death and resurrection of Christ. The noon dining table was covered with china, dyed eggs, napkins, and candles in pastel. Ceramic bunnies and other spring creatures surrounded small crystal vases filled with flowers. Other spring creatures provided a festive centerpiece. We were delighted when Alan and Karen invited friends without family in town to join us for Easter dinner. Karen served a traditional Easter meal, complete with ham and coconut cake.

Celebrate at home with friends. We hosted an early spring retirement celebration last month. Lacy white invitations were handwritten in gold calligraphy. Three couples came to dinner on Friday night, and we greeted them in the den with appetizers surrounding a crystal vase of white tulips, all displayed on a lace-covered table. A gold and white arrangement of roses, lilies, and stock interspersed with freesia, smilix, and Boston fern sprayed with gold paint served as the centerpiece of the dining table. The arrangement was loosely encircled by strings of gold beads. Tall crystal candlesticks held marbled gold and white candles. The dining table was covered with the best white lace cloth, gold chargers, white china, and sparkling crystal. Each place setting of silver was partially enclosed in a fan-folded napkin tied with gold wire ribbon and placed on each charger. The host and hostess served the food. The spring evening literally blossomed as friends chatted while the taped orchestra played Vivaldi's "Spring" from the *Four Seasons*.

PRACTICAL POINTERS

Enjoy every blooming plant in your house and yard. Invite friends, your Sunday school class, or a neighbor for lunch. Pick the last pansies for your centerpiece. If you are replacing your pansies with summer bedding plants, pot the healthiest pansies in small inexpensive clay containers for your kitchen window or the window of a friend. Cut the first rose of the season and take it to a neighbor, shut-in, or someone who is ill.

Perhaps you don't have flowers in your yard. Take a look around your neighborhood or your city. From nurseries to home improvement centers, from garden centers to stands beside the roads, cities are literally blooming with inexpensive plants. Flowers become instruments of love when used to reach out to others, on Easter, Mother's Day, even Father's Day.

Several years ago the women of our church sponsored a conference entitled "Bloom Where You Are Planted." Every spring I am reminded of this concept. Each of us in our particular place and at the appropriate time has opportunities to bloom. Flowers display their beauty where they are planted—and each of us has unique opportunities to reach out to those around us with an expression of love and beauty. The beauty of flowers is fleeting, and likewise, our window of opportunity to meet a need in the life of another can rarely be reclaimed.

The husband of our "couple friends" had surgery last week. I talked to him yesterday and told him we would come by this weekend to visit. I had planned to make a coffee cake, but spring is not coffee cake season. I think we will take a rosebush to Bob instead. Spring is a time for everything—and everyone—to blossom.

GLIMPSES
Like the sun,
love radiates and warms into life
all that it touches.

O. S. MARDEN

Summer Celebrations

Be still, and know that I am God. . . .

PSALM 46:10 KJV

Children run barefoot and giggle as they splash through water under outside sprinkler systems. Gulf Coast beaches are covered with sunbathers. The musical sound of an ice cream truck attracts young and old alike. Summer has arrived.

At our house the American flag flies from the front yard flagpole. Cars line the driveway and the curb in front of our home. The aroma of grilled chicken, pork ribs, and barbecue sauce announces to each arriving guest that we are celebrating Independence Day, the Fourth of July, the birthday of our country. July is hot and humid in the South, so at our house this traditional family gathering is held inside.

Our regular crew is made up of local family members, friends without family in Mobile, and occasionally our out-of-town adult children and families. Everyone brings something delicious to serve with our barbecued meat. It is a simple lazy, hazy day; a time to relax, sing a patriotic song, or read a poem about our homeland. Everyone reminisces and repeats stories each of us wants to hear at least one more time. The pound cake, iced in white and trimmed with red and blue, is covered with miniature flags. Each of us weighs a little heavier on the scales at the end of a day of fellowship, but we feel a little lighter inside.

Many of us associate summer with a slower paced lifestyle. Even if both parents are still working, at least there is no homework and lunches to pack for children. Summer is an opportunity to slow the pace, to do something family centered.

PRACTICAL POINTERS

- Consider creating a "Sunday dinner" for your family, the kind you enjoyed as a child. Fry

chicken and make gravy, mash some potatoes, and cook some homegrown vegetables.
Double the amount that you need for your
own family and invite church friends to join
you. You might invite someone who is
unchurched to your Sunday morning service
and then to dinner at your house. If you're
not much of a cook or if you're short on time,
you could cook fresh vegetables and pick up
spicy chicken from a famous fast-food
restaurant. Your guests would enjoy the time
together, even if the chicken arrives in a box!

- Summers often revolve around vacations. If
you vacation, plan a theme party using ideas
from the location you visited. If you aren't
going anywhere, pretend you have been to
Hawaii or another exotic location and use that
theme for your party. Use outdated posters
from travel agencies and decorations from
party stores. Once I planned a summer luncheon using the theme from some clever invitations I found on a sale table at a card shop.

- Invite neighborhood children for an hour-
long backyard Vacation Bible School each
morning for a week. Enlist the help of older

teens from your church to help with stories, Bible skits, and games. Something as simple as returning thanks at snack time might touch the heart of a child. Send a note home with each child on the final day and an invitation for the family to visit your church services.

- Plan an outside-inside picnic using inexpensive red-and-white-checked plastic table covers available in party supply stores. Washable quilts make nostalgic picnic table coverings. Decorate the tables with old-fashioned dolls, games, or other items you recall taking with you on childhood picnics.

- Purchase a bag of sand from your local hardware store (less than five dollars) and pour mounds of sand on each table to create ant beds. Buy packages of tiny plastic ants and bugs also found in party stores. Make a trail from the corner of the table to the mounds of sand with the tiny ants. Small plastic bugs can crawl everywhere, even on the edge of the plates of one or two adventuresome guests. Use a wicker picnic basket filled with potted plants as a centerpiece. Serve barbecued chicken, baked beans, slaw, and rolls. Or hotdogs, sandwiches, and chips on paper plates and Kool-Aid in plastic cups. Homemade cookies are a must for any picnic whether inside or out.

- Have an indoor picnic when the weather is rainy. Set up game tables inside for children or adults. Use plastic bugs (different bugs or different colors) for a game of checkers. The winner of a Scrabble game might be the person who spelled the longest—or the most unique—picnic word. Taped bird sounds add authentic atmosphere.

- Play hopscotch outside on the driveway. A simple table becomes an outside lemonade stand by attaching a sign that announces "Lemonade FREE today." Crank a freezer of your favorite ice cream and serve in paper cups as your guests gather around.

- Move the picnic site to a neighborhood park. Invite families to bring a basket filled with food to be shared. Children enjoy the playground equipment while parents visit. Almost everyone loves old-fashioned summer hospitality.

- Put away your "to do" list for a few days. Call a friend. Go to lunch. Read an inspirational

book. Enjoy a lazy day. Renew yourself.
When you are refreshed, reach out to
someone who might be experiencing the
"dog days" of summer.

GLIMPSES

*Teach me the art of
creating islands. . . ,
in which I can absorb
the beauty of everyday things.*

MARIAN STROUD

Celebrate Autumn— A Season of Thanksgiving

We always thank God for all of you,
mentioning you in our prayers.
1 Thessalonians 1:2 NIV

In early October Mark and Debbi phoned to invite us for a weekend with them in Birmingham, a four-hour drive from our home on the Alabama coast. They wanted to introduce us to their family October tradition, a trip to the "Pumpkin Patch." We were delighted with the invitation to visit with our adult children, enjoy our five-year-old grandson, and get the latest update on "Sarah," scheduled to make her debut in mid-December.

The Pumpkin Patch, located in a rural area

north of Birmingham, is a farm planted with dozens, maybe hundreds, of acres of pumpkins. Each year it opens its gates to visitors, mostly dads and moms who bring their children to ride in wagons to distant fields. The children and adults (including grandparents) comb the field looking for the best-shaped pumpkin. For one small fee, they pick their pumpkin of choice and take it home with them.

In addition to our pumpkin patch trek, we enjoyed a picnic lunch under a covered pavilion with entertainment by musicians and square dancers. Later, we bought jelly and preserves in the country store, and we found beautiful homegrown okra and tomatoes for sale outside under the trees.

We met the family who owned the farm. After a near-fatal accident, the Christian husband felt he had been given a "second life." He wanted to do something meaningful, something to touch the lives of others, so he bought the land and built the farm, a "return to yesteryear, a wholesome place for families to gather."

This is an annual day outing for our son and his family. By the end of October, the carved pumpkins are displayed on the front steps of their home to greet small hobgoblins that arrive for a Halloween treat.

Perhaps you don't have a pumpkin farm in your area. Find a produce stand or a pumpkin display at the grocery store. Buy one pumpkin per family and invite neighbors over for a Pumpkin Carving Party. When Halloween is over, store the pumpkin pulp in the refrigerator for a bake-off the next week. Wives return on the bake day with their assigned ingredient: sugar, eggs, milk, or spices. Everyone brings two unbaked pie shells. Bake and deliver half of the warm pumpkin pies to shut-ins, widows, or new neighbors—saving one per family for the night's dessert.

Autumn—a time to count blessings. One of these is my favorite day of all, the longest day of the year—the only day with twenty-five hours, the day we set our clocks back after the summer months of Daylight Savings Time.

Autumn—a time to enjoy leaves coated with a seemingly endless array of color dumped from a gigantic heavenly bucket of paint, the crisp mornings and warm Indian summer afternoons, the smell of marshmallows and wieners roasting outside.

Autumn—a time to celebrate and give thanks, as

did our pioneer ancestors, for the bountiful blessings of the harvest. A time to consider inviting others into our home.

My calendar reminds me autumn has arrived. The air is crisp and often smells like cinnamon. Leaves are changing in the Deep South and turkeys are an endangered species. We are buying cranberry sauce and planning our Thanksgiving holiday celebration.

Those of you who read my book *Mama's Home-made Love* recall I inherited the family Thanksgiving celebration many years ago. What began as my mother's family get-together when I was a child evolved into a large gathering at my mother's house. After my father's premature death, my mother passed the Thanksgiving holiday torch to me. Thirty years later, Don and I continue to host the daylong celebration each fourth Thursday in November.

The guest list has changed over the years. We now invite family friends to join us for the day—widows, longtime family friends with no in-town children, friends whose family lives away, and others who have no one with whom they share holidays. One invitation gives lifetime membership to each extended family gathering. When our homes are filled with people we know, they are filled with love.

Change is constant and most of the older generation has passed on to a place of greater celebration. Last Thanksgiving Day was the first holiday season I recall being separated from a special cousin; her tragic condition did not allow her to attend. At first I didn't want to get together this year at all if she couldn't be there; it would be too painful. Then I quickly realized that we didn't have a choice. Many individuals and couples would spend the day alone if we did not continue our family tradition, the tradition we lovingly call our "Orphan Party."

If *you* don't get a better invitation, you are invited to our house on Thanksgiving Day. Give us a call. We can always find an extra place at our table. We just need enough time to print your name on a place card and find another plate. We always provide the turkey, dressing, gravy, and cranberry sauce. If you like, you can bring your favorite casserole. Time? By midmorning folks will begin gathering, and many stay for a turkey sandwich, coffee, and dessert late in the evening.

PRACTICAL POINTERS

Plan a holiday celebration of your own. Invite your extended family and maybe a few friends. Include one or more people who would be otherwise left alone on the special day. If you are widowed, invite other widowed friends who won't be spending the holiday with their own families. Young couples who are geographically separated from family at this season can invite a couple, or several couples, to bring children and food for the day.

A beautiful example of hospitality was shared with me recently when I spoke to a church group. More than half the church was made up of seniors, many of whom lived lonely lives. One young church couple (with three pre-schoolers) cannot spend every holiday with family in distant cities, so each year the couple plans a Senior Celebration for their in-town holiday. Invitations are sent to all senior church members. Everyone brings their choice of casserole, rolls, drinks, or paper products.

Thrilled that this young couple was reaching out

to others, I commended this young mother. "This is a unique hospitality idea," I said. "It must be such a blessing to those who are invited."

"Oh, the blessing is ours," she replied. "We enjoy our guests tremendously. They are such a source of wisdom to me—and to my husband. It's like having lots of parents nearby. And it is an opportunity for my children to get grandparent hugs every time we go to church."

As a demonstration of God's love and blessing in your life, open your home during this Thanksgiving season. Give of yourself to others who are less fortunate, lonely, or hurting. When you do so without any expectation of reward, you will receive the greatest blessing!

GLIMPSES

I awoke this morning with
devout thanksgiving for my friends,
the old and the new.
Shall I not call God, the Beautiful,
who daily showeth Himself
so to me in His gifts.

RALPH WALDO EMERSON

Celebrate the Real Meaning of the Christmas Season

And the Word became flesh, and dwelt among us,
and we beheld His glory,
glory as of the only begotten from the Father,
full of grace and truth.

JOHN 1:14 NASB

The day was busy yet relaxing, exhausting but paradoxically exhilarating. For eight hours our home was filled with family, friends, food, laughter, and love. Don and I caught our breath after the last guest left and reflected on the day. We were thankful for another successful Thanksgiving celebration.

Then we began what we call "our magic act," scurrying around getting everything back in place. We loaded the dishwasher with the last dirty dishes, stored the leftover food, and pulled out the vacuum. We were tired, but we both wanted to get the house back to normal as quickly as possible.

A short time later everything was done. We just stood back and admired our efforts for a few moments. Tomorrow would be a new day, another adventure. We could start that day fresh—and the house was in order!

Don collapsed into his recliner and picked up the remote control, hoping to catch the last play of the *big* game. (Wife's definition of *big* game: "Any game currently being televised.")

There was one more thing I wanted to do. I knew Don would think it foolish, but my tired body still hummed with excitement, and I knew I had to do it. I pulled a chair up to the china cabinet, climbed onto the chair, and carefully lifted eight china Christmas plates off the top shelf. I retrieved cups and saucers and every piece of the Christmas china, and then I covered the freshly polished dining table with the Christmas china, crystal, and silver—still warm from the dishwasher.

Like a little girl, I could not wait another minute

after serving the last slice of Thanksgiving pie to begin celebrating one of my favorite seasons of the year, Christmas. There is something special about Christmas, an excitement, and there should be—Christmas celebrates the birth of the Savior of the world.

Sadly, as in other situations in today's fast-paced world, many people have lost their focus at Christmastime. Even Christians have lost their focus. What happens in our society during the month of December has little to do with the birth of a Savior in a stable.

When the Christmas season arrives this year, I challenge you to return to the stable, to listen to the beautiful music of angels, and to look into the face of a tiny infant whose life changed the course of history. Christmas should be a time of rejoicing in His birth— the perfect time for Christians to reach out to others with a message of hope and love.

"But," you might ask, "how can I be expected to do anything more than survive amid the frenzied activity that accompanies this holy season? If you are going to ask me to do more, the answer is no. I am peddling as fast as I can." I would not ask anyone to do more; most of the world, like you, pedals at full speed year-round.

When I was a young mother, a wise older friend told me that each of us finds time to do the things we really want to do, that which is truly important to us. We make choices. We decide what is important and those things become our priorities.

Today many Christians follow a distorted priority list. Many find their list becomes even more distorted during the Christmas season as we frantically run from task to task. The ritual of giving gifts results in overspending on gifts for people who have so much "stuff" there is nothing left they need. We rush from event to event, and at best we only half enjoy what we are doing. Simultaneously, we are frantically making plans we hope will allow us to survive the next day in this glorious season. If you see yourself in this picture, look a little more closely. I stand beside you, guilty as charged.

Thirty years ago I heard a compelling story that became the inspiration for the rest of this chapter. It is with gratitude to the unknown author that I offer to you a fictional version of a Christmas dinner at our house (and perhaps your house) when our children were young.

This was my year to do everything right. Our family would have the perfect Christmas, since Don's raise allowed us to buy nicer gifts. The tree would be larger and more beautiful; Santa would be more generous; Christmas dinner would be unhurried; and everyone would like his or her gifts.

Christmas morning actually went rather well. The temperature was below freezing and the wind was blustery. In the South we appreciate cold weather at Christmastime—even without snow. If the air is cold, it seems more like the Christmas pictured on the cards we receive from our northern friends. The boys expressed delight in the surprises Santa brought, and everyone was in a festive mood. Each dish I prepared looked delicious.

Just as the clock struck twelve, I lit the candles on the dining table and we bowed our heads. The family gave thanks for the food. . .and all our other blessings. Amen. I felt so blessed—*finally* we were having a "Walton Christmas"!

No sooner had we finished the blessing, when we heard a soft knock at the front door. "This is not the time for *anyone* to visit," I thought. "Who in this world would be so inconsiderate as to arrive unexpectedly on Christmas Day?"

Don unlocked the door, and a puzzled look crept across his face. Outside the partially opened door, I saw a man dressed in strange clothing. I couldn't hear what he was saying, but I heard Don inviting him to come inside where it was warm. The man seemed reluctant—he really didn't want to interrupt our family holiday dinner, he said. Meanwhile he clutched his cloak close to his body, shivering in the frigid outside temperature. Don's genuine insistence convinced him to come inside, warm his body, and sit with us at our table.

He was different, yet we were not fearful of this stranger. His eyes were kind, and he spoke softly. He seemed personally interested in each of us, almost as if he knew us. Strangely, we felt the same way about him. After he finished a warm cup of tea, I offered him a plate, and he filled it with food. He seemed comfortable and told us that he appreciated our hospitality.

I realized the children would expect to open gifts, as was our tradition after dinner each Christmas Day. I excused myself and left the room to search for something, anything, I could wrap quickly for our guest. "He must have a gift to open," I said softly to myself. It didn't seem right for everyone except our guest to have a gift. The extra box of handkerchiefs somehow didn't seem appropriate. I had noticed he was wearing sandals, and I found some warm socks—but then I decided that wasn't the right gift either. Each of us would be opening something *nice*.

In desperation I grabbed a book on the real meaning of Christmas, the birth of Jesus, wrapped it and tied a pretty bow. It wasn't an expensive book, but it did have a good message. This would just have to do. After all, we had not expected him to be with us for Christmas dinner. If only he had let us know he wanted to come to our house for Christmas, we could have bought him a really nice gift.

When I returned to the dining room, Mark was sitting in the stranger's lap, listening intently as he told a story about sheep, shepherds, and love. I had the strongest feeling I had seen a picture in the past of that same man telling stories to little children. When he finished the story, Mark slid down from his lap. The visitor said he needed to be on his way, but the children begged him to stay with us as we opened gifts. We exchanged gifts, but each of us was focused on our guest. The packages we had so anticipated opening lost most of their significance in the presence of this stranger.

When we gave the stranger his gift last, we couldn't tell if he was pleased. For just a moment he had a sad, faraway look in his eyes. *Perhaps he has already read the book,* I thought. Then he told us he needed to be on his way and again thanked us for food and warmth, for hospitality.

As he started out the door, he turned back for a moment. He talked so softly we were not certain, but each of us thought we heard him say, "Today is my birthday." We huddled together on the cold porch and watched until he disappeared around the corner. Our hearts were suddenly sad and lonely as we realized the truth: The guest of honor had left our Christmas celebration.

Have we forgotten whose birthday we celebrate at Christmastime? How many years have we celebrated Christmas without acknowledging the One whose birthday we remember? Take a moment to consider how you might feel if the Stranger from Galilee rings your doorbell on the twenty-fifth of December this year. I'm not asking that you do anything more than take your considerations seriously. I'm certainly not asking you to do more at Christmastime; perhaps you even need to do less.

PRACTICAL POINTERS

Decide on one or two things you will do that will make Christmas more Christ-centered, things that will make a difference in the life of someone you know. Pattern yourself after the example of Jesus' life. Use the birthday of Christ as an opportunity to reach out to others.

GLIMPSES

*Each of us must actively draw near to God at Christmas.
Caught up in the holiday season, we easily let our devotional life slip and even forget temporarily about religious things.
But a Christ-centered, merry Christmas is not likely to come automatically.
It comes when we plan ahead and deliberately make room for Christ in our holiday celebrations.*

GARY COLLINS

Celebrating the Season with Less Fuss

He who refreshes others will himself be refreshed.
PROVERBS 11:25 NIV

On the day after "Turkey Day," I can hardly wait to finish my morning coffee sipped from a china Christmas mug. The Christmas season officially arrived last night when I pulled those plates off the top shelf in the china cabinet. Today is special.

I will decorate the Christmas tree. The shopping is done (well almost), and wrapped packages will be retrieved from where I stored them last summer. (I prefer to buy gifts no later than early fall.) A decorated tree without gifts is like a wrapped package before the bow is tied.

If all goes well (and I have a little help from my husband), by bedtime tonight I may have candles in the windows, nativity scenes on the tables, and even stockings by the fireplace. Once the house is decorated, the Christmas spirit just creeps in and I begin to relax. Now I look forward to enjoying the season, baking fruitcakes, having friends over, visiting in their homes, and rejoicing in the birth of the Savior.

Right? Yes, right. Well, maybe. But we *must* rejoice. If the lost world cannot see a difference in the lives of Christians during this special season, perhaps it is time for us to take a closer look at those things that need to be changed to make that difference more obvious. Any small step we make toward the manger can make a dramatic difference in our December days.

Hang on. Keep turning pages. What you read is not fiction. I have practical suggestions to offer to you—but only if you want to simplify the Christmas season.

If you love the Christmas season as much as I do, you won't mind shopping and wrapping before summer's end, baking and freezing early, or trimming the tree and decorating the house the day after Thanksgiving. Some of these ideas and suggestions I offer are things I have done for years. I know they work. Others? Well, I am trying to improve each year.

When Don and I make our individual and family goals on New Year's, I find a blank page in the back of my calendar and begin my Christmas/birthday gift list. Each family member is listed, leaving adequate space for gifts to be entered beneath the names. Often I will write down several ideas I picked up listening to the children talk during the holidays.

"Mom, I loved the shirt. You know I don't like to spend money on clothes for myself," Alan said. "Anytime you find a shirt you think I will like, buy it. I can always use another Sunday shirt." Last January when I entered Alan's name on the Christmas list, I wrote "Sunday shirt." The list of ideas has grown considerably. When a purchase is made, the item is highlighted or circled. At the mall or on a trip, I recognize who needs shopping attention with one glance. Often the reminder from the list results in a special gift for someone at a reduced price. It just takes a few minutes to occasionally update the list—much less time than pulling bags out of a closet because I can't remember what I bought for whom!

Christmas gifts are special, symbolic of love. Symbolism quickly turns to chaos, though, when we shop late, overspend, frantically wrap, and agonize when the credit card statement arrives in January. I experience my greatest Christmas pressure when the shopping is not completed early.

PRACTICAL POINTERS

If you want to simplify the season, make a reasonable and attainable goal for your shopping completion date. Share your goal with several friends who might like to simplify their season. Somehow it makes us accountable when we tell another person our plans. If they like the idea, grab the calendars and plan a "Gift Wrap Get-Together." Write the date and time on your calendar—no later than the middle of October.

Call to remind everyone two weeks prior to the date. Not everyone will be finished shopping, but everyone surely will have something to wrap. If not, the impetus of the upcoming wrapping event may motivate your friends.

Use the largest floor space you have. You will need it. Have everyone bring gift wrap, tape, ribbon, tags, and boxes. Serve simple refreshments— for instance, sugar cookies with red and green

sprinkles on top—on Christmas plates. Dig out
Christmas tapes and leftover Christmas napkins.

After your friends leave, stand back and
admire your handiwork before you store the gifts.
When I put my gifts away, I always have a warm
feeling as I think about wrapped packages hidden
on the top shelf of the closet or underneath a bed.
It's a half-secret, half-smug kind of feeling.

Most people I ask agree three major pressures are asso-
ciated with Christmas: gift buying, decorations, and food
preparation. Eliminating these three pressures allows us
to participate in—and even enjoy—the activities of the
season.

We have already solved the gift-buying mania.
Now try decorating your tree and your house the weekend after Thanksgiving. I will feel honored if you use my
idea. And once you do, you will likely continue to be one
of the first in your neighborhood each year to turn on
Christmas lights.

But, you ask, what about food? Our grand-
mothers had no choice; everything was from scratch,

involving time-consuming hard work over a hot stove. Each bite tasted great and was made with love. I still love that *idea*, but I do little of that intensive cooking during the Christmas season. Instead, I make and freeze gumbo, serve a traditional Christmas dinner, and make at least one homemade dessert—but only for my family. During this busy season everyone else is served something that just *might* have been purchased at the grocery deli, a wholesale warehouse, or picked up at a local bakery or doughnut shop.

With such an abundance of prepared food available, I spend as little time as possible in the kitchen during the holiday season. Rather, I use other less hurried (or perhaps, as some say, less harried) times during the year to lovingly prepare for guests in our home.

In just a few short pages, your Christmas preparation list has been made as easy as A, B, C, or perhaps, B, D, and C (Buy and wrap, Decorate, and Celebrate—with prepared food).

These ideas are not for everyone. I have friends who appear to actually enjoy finishing their shopping as the doors are locked on Christmas Eve, putting the tree up at midnight, and arising at daylight to bake corn bread for dressing.

However, if you, like me, long for less stress and more joy, a time to visit with friends, a time to open doors at home, then the word is *simplify*. When we do, we can find new meaning in celebrating the birth of the One who gave us life.

This Christmas give it a try. Simplify your life. Simplify the season.

GLIMPSES
Simplicity, simplicity, simplicity!
I say let your affairs be as two or three,
and not a hundred or a thousand.

HENRY DAVID THOREAU

Simple
Christmas Celebrations

How beautiful on the mountains
are the feet of those who bring good news,
who proclaim peace, who bring good tidings,
who proclaim salvation, who say to Zion,
"Your God reigns!"
ISAIAH 52:7 NIV

Last December twenty-third I called my friend Ada Pearl to wish her a merry Christmas. You may recall meeting her in *Mama's Homemade Love* as she prepared Mama's Saturday night supper for me one Monday. This time she was busy in the kitchen, as usual, cooking supper and preparing treats for carolers who would come by later in the evening. *Christmas carolers,* I mused, *are live individuals standing outside homes announcing musically, as did the angels, the birth of the Savior.*

It had been years since I last heard carolers singing outside at Christmastime. We were enjoying a festive night in the home of a friend. The turn-of-the-century home was furnished with antiques and filled with friends celebrating the Christmas season around a gigantic tree. Outside the air was "bitterly cold," a term we rarely have opportunity to use in Mobile.

Guests heard a faint sound of bells, followed by the voices of carolers. For the next ten minutes, party guests were mesmerized by a small group of warmly dressed neighbors standing on the front steps of the home. Snowflakes, yes real-from-heaven snowflakes, gently landed on their faces and the steps where they stood as they sang about a holy night and a tiny Baby born two thousand years ago. After my own quiet "moment in time," the carolers disappeared into the darkness, making their way to the home next door.

Now, I listened to Ada Pearl tell about the caroling tradition at her church. For many years she had participated, but she is older now. Tonight she and her husband would stay home and the carolers would come to them to sing and perhaps enjoy cookies and a warm drink. Union Baptist Church of rural Grand Bay continues its longtime simple Christmas celebration of carols outside homes in this south Mobile County community.

After we said good-bye, I continued to reflect on carolers. During the first half of this century the Christmas season meant that neighbors, friends, and church groups reached out in love as they sang carols on the front lawn or steps of homes. What in this world has happened? Perhaps when we locked the front door and no longer welcomed friends inside, we lost a simple yet powerful means of touching lives. Today the word "caroler" has been reduced to a Christmas decoration, a ceramic or papier-mâché group of warmly dressed individuals with songbooks standing beside a lamppost.

This lost tradition might be one you could rekindle during the next Christmas season. Ask a few friends, neighbors, choir members, or children from your church to join your family one evening prior to Christmas. Sing to neighbors, shut-ins, or nursing home residents.

Holidays, traditionally, are times to visit with friends. We can simplify without losing our holiday traditions. Rather than planning an elaborate dinner party this Christmas season, consider small and simple gatherings, occasions for fellowship with family and friends, chances to reach out to others in love. Set aside a night to string cranberries or popcorn for an old-fashioned tree. Begin a new family tradition. Traditions make holidays, especially Christmas, a warm and comfortable time.

Call several couples and invite them to come to "Christmas Past" at your house. Ask guests to bring a picture of their family made during any past Christmas season. Maybe they could also bring a finger food served by their grandparents or something they traditionally serve during the season in their own homes. When the day arrives, mix the spice tea you will serve to your guests. Add the aroma of scented candles. Build a fire in the fireplace and turn on the traditional Christmas music. Encourage families to share pictures, special memories of "Christmas Past," and the story of the snack they brought.

If you are past fifty, locate someone with an old mesh stocking sold during the fifties and fill it with small toys and hard candy. Tell the group about the simplicity of Christmas during this era. Or watch *A Christmas Carol* on videotape. Invite your guests to attend a Christmas music presentation or other special events at your church.

The same idea could be used for "Christmas

Present," with couples sharing traditions they brought into the home and new traditions they began after marriage. A guest from another culture would add an interesting dimension. "Christmas Future" would likely spark creative conversation as the group speculates how the world might celebrate the birth of Christ one hundred years into the future.

PRACTICAL POINTERS

Simple Ways to Say "Happy Birthday, Jesus":

- Invite your children or grandchildren's friends to your house to celebrate the birthday of Christ. Allow the children to decorate an iced cake with candles. Sing "Happy Birthday" to Jesus. Read the Christmas story from the Bible or a favorite children's book. Simple props—a doll, blanket, housecoats, and gifts—allow the children to reenact the events. Sing-along tapes provide an opportunity for wee guests to participate.
- If the Nutcracker Ballet is performed in your city, take a daughter or a granddaughter.

Invite her friends to come to your home for
tea after the performance. Use nutcrackers
for the centerpiece on the tea table. Serve the
young ladies sugar cookies and tea sipped
from china cups (but not those that would
make you cry if one was accidentally
dropped!).

Fond Christmas memories from the era when our children were young are simple: buying and decorating the
Christmas tree; a traditional Christmas Eve breakfast
that included another family; visiting with the neighborhood granny, Ma-Ma Cammon, for punch, peanut
butter cookies, and sometimes a homemade stuffed toy
or other gift. The ideas are simple, yet the memories
warm our hearts many years later.

We plan to do something simple during the upcoming holiday season. We plan to host a Saturday morning group in early December. We have lived in Bienville
Woods for years and only recently during Mobile by
Candlelight met some of our closest neighbors. Christmas
is still months away, but we plan to have a "coffee" at our

house. We will invite not only those who live on our street, but also other couples in the subdivision, just a comfortable number to visit and drink coffee. We will not have breakfast, brunch, or lunch. Just coffee—and orange juice. Maybe a few hot doughnut holes, some Christmas music, and a time to visit.

Ralph Waldo Emerson said it best. "The only true gift is a gift of yourself." So this year we will simplify and just give a part of ourselves, time, love—and coffee.

GLIMPSES

If we too are wise,
we will bring the Christ Child our
hearts' greatest treasures,
laying them down at His feet with
worship and love and wonder.

ELLYN SANNA,
Christmas at Home

Passing the Torch

Train the younger women. . . .
TITUS 2:4 NIV

Just three days after Christmas I received a chicken salad 911 call. My friend Lee needed my chicken salad recipe to serve to a schoolmate who was coming to lunch. I recited the recipe from memory. I make it often, so I know *about* how much to use of each ingredient.

She only asked for a recipe, but I gave her more information than she needed, and perhaps more than she wanted. We talked about serving the salad on a lacy lettuce leaf, perhaps with a croissant or warm sourdough bread roll. "Add a fruit salad and poppy-seed dressing," I said. "And what do you have that you can use for a favor? A bookmark would be appropriate for a student. Don't forget some soft seasonal music. You two need to relax before you begin another semester." I knew that she would do everything and more to make her friend feel special.

PRACTICAL POINTERS

For a change, try this recipe for Southwestern chicken salad:

2 whole cooked chicken breasts, shredded or diced
1 small red onion, minced
2 plum tomatoes, diced
1 ripe avocado, peeled and diced
½ cup fresh cilantro, minced

¼ cup olive oil
¼ cup fresh lime juice
½ tsp grated lime zest
1 tsp cumin
chili powder to taste
salt and pepper to taste

Combine and refrigerate for at least 1 hour to allow flavors to blend.

Lee has a unique way of touching lives. She tells me I have been an inspiration to her. Now I watch as she opens her own home, offering love and hospitality.

In 1957 I was newly married and had mastered, with the help of many kind souls, a few kitchen survival skills. And now I was ready to learn to bake a pie. I had made a graham cracker crust filled with pudding mix topped with whipped cream pie, but now I wanted to make a real pie with homemade crust and cooked filling covered with meringue, swirled high and baked golden brown.

About this same time we had a covered dish supper at church. Mrs. McElhanney, a newcomer to town and to our church, brought a homemade cooked-from-scratch lemon pie. The crust was "melt in your mouth flaky," filled with lemon custard and topped with swirls of meringue. I complimented Mrs. McElhanney and told her I wanted to learn to make a pie like hers.

She quickly asked, "Can you come to my house next Tuesday? My daughter is not interested in learning to cook, but I can teach you how to make a pie! We'll just make pies together."

The next Tuesday I arrived on her steps with my bag of flour, shortening, Pyrex pie plate, and an assortment of other pie-making utensils and ingredients. Mrs. McElhanney opened her door and reached out to me in love. We worked side by side at her kitchen table, cutting the shortening into the flour and adding iced water to make dough. Then we rolled the creation into a circular sheet of thin, stiff dough the size of a plate.

I learned a lot about hospitality that day. An older woman (anyone past forty was an older woman to me at the time) took time to mentor someone half her age who wanted to make a pie. We cooked lemon custard, beat egg whites into stiff peaks, and browned the swirled meringue. She served lunch, and we sampled her pie. Later that afternoon I left her house with my first real homemade pie and a warm feeling inside.

The McElhanneys moved away and we lost touch, but not before she had passed a hospitality torch to another generation. It wasn't all about pie that day— it was more about touching the life of a young wife.

Within two years I was a student sitting at the feet of another godly woman who opened her heart to me when my first child was born. She was our pastor's wife with four children of her own and many church roles to fill. But her door was always open.

Sprawling oak trees surrounded her home and a wide front porch stretched from side to side of her house. I sat in a swing on that porch for hours while our firstborn, Alan, slept in my arms. On damp, cold, winter afternoons, Mrs. Dossett made a fire, and we drank hot chocolate while the baby played at my feet. I savored bits of wisdom from one who took time to open her heart in love. I realized, too late to thank her, that she taught me a lot about children and life, but she taught me even more about hospitality.

Perhaps I can measure to some degree the effect Mrs. McElhanney had on me whenever I make a piecrust. Or, watching my own children parent, I can give some credit to Mrs. Dossett. But less tangible and more difficult to measure is the effect of a door that opened to me when I was a nine-year-old child. How can I measure the impact of another dear saint who taught me to memorize and love the Scriptures?

Mrs. Lillian McFadyen opened her front door once each week for almost four years and invited me to enter. I sat on her couch and memorized verses for the Junior Bible Drill held each year in Baptist churches. She listened as I recited, prompted when I forgot, and encouraged me to learn the Scriptures letter perfect. Meanwhile, she cooked supper for a family of four in her tiny kitchen just a few feet from the couch where I sat.

Opening one's home to a child may seem insignificant to many. But I am the person I am today because of the power of God's Word. Most of the Scripture I recite from memory I learned on a weekly basis when a Sunday school teacher offered hospitality to a skinny, stringy-haired kid.

Reflecting on these three and countless others who opened their hearts and homes to me, I am humbled that they invested precious time and Christian love to help me reach toward my God-given potential. How can I thank them?

Each of us has a Mrs. McElhanney, a Mrs. Dossett, or a Mrs. McFadyen. You call yours other names and perhaps they reached out to you in different ways, but you know who they are and you know the difference they made in your life. How can you thank them?

Pray that God will give you a renewed love for family, friends, neighbors, and yes, even strangers. Open your doors. Give to others what was freely given to you. Allow others to experience your hospitality and thus receive the torch from you. Send another generation forth holding hospitality torches high as they march confidently into the new millennium!

GLIMPSES
One can never pay in gratitude;
one can only pay "in kind"
somewhere else in life.

ANNE MORROW LINDBERGH

A Servant's Heart

Be imitators of God, therefore,
as dearly loved children and live a life of love,
just as Christ loved us and gave himself up for us
as a fragrant offering and sacrifice to God.

EPHESIANS 5:1–2 NIV

Through the soft light of the early morning hour, the wife watched her husband struggle to put on his shoes. His slight physical limitations made this a difficult task each workday morning. Then, after working eight or ten hours, he returned home, facing the same difficulty as he removed his high-top Wolverines.

One afternoon the wife knelt in front of his chair and began unlacing her husband's shoes. She carefully removed first his shoes and then his socks. His feet were dirty and sweaty after hours of toil. He questioned, "Why did you do that for me?"

"You struggle each morning to put those shoes on so you can go out into the world and earn our living. When you return, you are tired. I want to show my appreciation to you by removing your shoes." She continued to do this each day of his forty-five-year work career—a dramatic display of love and gratitude. In this true story, a wife with a loving heart willingly became a servant as she daily removed her husband's smelly shoes.

We are each born with a selfish nature. Those with changed hearts become servants as they follow in the footsteps of Christ.

My mother enrolled me in the "Cradle Roll" at church, and I was considered a member of Sunday school even before I entered the church building. In foggy memories I recall navigating from plank to plank through the muddy construction site at Dauphin Way Baptist Church in Mobile, Alabama. Before my fourth birthday, wartime rationing of gasoline dictated that we attend a church closer to home. We went to church twice each Sunday and many weekdays. I think my mother must have believed in eleven commandments, with the last one addressing church attendance.

I can't remember a time I didn't know about Jesus and believe in God. I wanted to be obedient and do what was right (most of the time). When I was twelve years old, I went forward during a Sunday night worship service invitation, took the preacher's hand, joined the church, and was baptized. But it was many years later before I prayed to receive Christ as my Savior.

The conviction of the Holy Spirit had been strong for months, but my pride was even stronger. Lying beside my sleeping husband on a June Sunday night in 1961, I committed my heart to Christ. Confused and hurting, I silently prayed, "God, if I haven't been saved, I want to be now. I accept Your offer of salvation provided by the death of Jesus." I cried, then slept peacefully for the first time in months.

I awoke to a new world. The early-morning sunshine filtering through our bedroom window seemed brighter and the birds sounded sweeter. The grass looked greener and the sky was the most beautiful blue I could imagine. I saw my husband and my child through new eyes, and each became more precious. The Scriptures spoke to my heart, and now prayer, rather than a rote recitation, was an ongoing dialogue with God. I had a life-changing experience—a new heart.

Since that morning forty years ago, I have been on a "two steps forward, one step backward" journey of Christian growth. God has spoken to me through His Word, through godly friends, and through many preachers of the gospel. But it was a college chapel speaker (during one of the five times I returned to school as an adult) who made a statement that continues to be life-changing for me.

"Study the life of Christ. Use Him as your example. Make your goal for life simple—to live a Christlike life." This was a challenging statement. How could I know how Christ would act? I began to study the Scriptures.

For the first time I clearly saw Christ in the role of a servant. I wasn't sure I wanted to be one, though. I knew I wanted to be more loving, kind, and compassionate. I wanted to meet the needs of those around me and make a difference in a life—but a servant? Did I really want to be a servant?

One brief mental glimpse at my Savior on a cross giving His life blood for me, and I knew there could only be one answer.

PRACTICAL POINTERS

The Bible depicts hospitality as a lifestyle of willing service resulting from inner change. Acts of
service need not be dramatic. More often they are
simple. . . .

- picking up groceries for an elderly person,
- raking a yard,
- driving to a distant city to attend a funeral,
- sitting with a friend in a hospital awaiting
  the report of the surgeon,
- reading to someone in the nursing home,
- taking a pie across the street,
- washing dishes in a home where a family is
  experiencing the sting of death,
- taking cold drinks on a hot afternoon to
  young workers cutting a tree next door,
- or just opening the doors of your own home.

Those who know me best know I fail on a daily basis.
Some days I fail more miserably than other days. But

God speaks to me in His quiet voice and teaches me to listen. He knows I am busy, and He gently reminds me of things that are important in the big picture of life. When I am tired and do not respond to His call, I remember He has promised me rest when I am weary. God did not call me to a task that is too big for me. He knows my limitations, and He is patient. Even so, for me, the servant's role remains a daily struggle.

A friend told me about Maggie, a godly woman she met years ago. Maggie wore an apron everywhere she went, a habit she acquired when she was eight years old. The apron was part of her church attire. She offered this explanation. "I don't know who I am until I put my apron on." Perhaps each of us needs something tangible to remind us who we are. I think I do.

After the death of his grandmother, our son Mark was the recipient of a beautifully written letter of love and encouragement. Mark later learned that Lucille, a member of the congregation where he serves as a staff member, types a personal letter to each member of the large church family who experiences a death. She also arrives at the church office every Sunday morning to help in any way she is needed.

One mother of two teens finds employment that

allows her to be home each afternoon when her sons return from school. Homework time and preparing an evening meal for the family to eat together is a priority for this single mom. She opens her home to neighborhood youngsters who return from school to an empty apartment. Some "afternoon children" have accepted her invitation to attend activities at her church.

This morning I received a call from a friend whose mother had died recently. My friend is hurting, and she asked if we could meet for coffee and talk. The writer inside me had a plan for today, a chapter to write. But a not-so-quiet voice inside me chided, *You will ignore a friend who needs you today so that you can* write *about a servant's heart?*

The Master continues to be patient with me, and I still have many things to learn. I need to be more willing—more flexible. I need to be sensitive to the needs of others. Within myself I do not have the love necessary to be the servant I should be. Only through His love am I able to serve. I still need to be reminded of who I am, to whom I belong.

I continue to struggle daily. But for now I have to go. In just a little while I will meet my friend for coffee.

GLIMPSES

*Make me firm and steadfast
in good works,
and make me persevere in Thy service,
so that I may always live to please Thee,
Lord Jesus Christ.*

CLARE OF ASSISI

THE AUTHOR
Barbara Sims is the author of *Mama's Homemade Love* (Promise Press, 1999). She is a frequent speaker at seminars and churches. Barbara lives in Mobile, Alabama, with her husband, Don. Their family includes two adult sons, two daughters-in-love, and three grandchildren.

Also Available from Barbara Sims...

As a simple Southern woman, Mama never had much education or an overflowing bank account. But she had practical wisdom and joy in abundance. You'll find yourself smiling—maybe even chuckling out loud—as she bakes the world's best biscuits without a recipe, argues with a tricky piece of embroidery, and delights the entire community with her glorious flower garden. These stories, and many more, will transport you to Mama's world, where you can relax on the front porch and enjoy the neighborhood.

1-57748-578-5
hardback,
$12.99

AVAILABLE WHEREVER
BOOKS ARE SOLD.